I JUST DIDN'T KNOW THAT

Revd Neville Barker Cryer

*For David
with warm fraternal
greetings*

Neville Barker Cryer

Lewis Masonic

First published 1999
Reprinted 2002

ISBN 0 85318 219 1

Published by Lewis Masonic

an imprint of Ian Allan Publishing Ltd,
Hersham, Surrey KT12 4RG

Printed by Ian Allan Printing Ltd,
Hersham, Surrey KT12 4RG

British Library Cataloguing in Data.
A Catalogue record for this book is available
from the British Library.

By the same author
What Do You Know About The Royal Arch?
210mm x 148mm, 104pp, ISBN 0 85318 227 2

Contents

About the Author

Bro Neville Barker Cryer was born in Accrington in 1924 and educated at Manchester Grammar School and Oxford, where his studies were interrupted between 1942 and 1946 by military service. In 1948/49, after completing his first degree in history, he studied theology in Cambridge, being ordained in 1950. His first curacy was in Derby, followed by Ilkeston. He was initiated into the Mother Lodge of Derbyshire, Tyrian Lodge No 253, in December 1950. He is still a member and the second longest serving member on the roll. He later joined Wolseley Lodge No 1993 and was exalted in 1956 in Affability Chapter No 317, both at Bridge Street, Manchester. In 1960, he became vicar of a parish in East Croydon and was soon to become one of the founders, and Junior Warden, of Comet Lodge No 7710. Over the past 40 years Bro Cryer has held many positions of note within Freemasonry; these include, in 1974, being the Prestonian Lecturer and, in 1996-98, the Batham Lecturer. It is with pride that he became the first English Freemason to have held both official lecturer appointments. He has also been the W.M., Secretary and Editor of the Quatuor Coronati Lodge No 2076 and has just been W.M. of the Manchester Lodge of Masonic Research, No 5502. Outside Freemasonry, Bro Cryer became Home Secretary of the Conference of British Missionary Societies in October 1967. In 1970 he became the General Secretary – later General Director – of the British & Foreign Bible Society, a post from which he retired in 1986. Twice married and now resident in York, Bro Cryer continues his active involvement in Freemasonry as he approaches the 50th anniversary of membership of the craft.

Introduction

For some years now, I have been invited to lecture in lodges not only across the length and breadth of England, but in many other parts of the British Isles and Ireland, as well as overseas. In undertaking these visits, I have been aware that there are probably two main kinds of audience. There are those who, even after several years in the Craft, have never really stopped to ask themselves about even the most obvious features of Freemasonry and who now want to learn something at a quite ordinary level. Why a lodge is called a lodge; why we have different kinds of clothing; what certain parts of the ritual really mean; these are the kinds of thing that come up repeatedly.

The other kind of audience is of a rather more advanced type that calls itself a Study Circle, a Research lodge, or even a Conference on Masonic subjects. The questions here have to do with the origins of Masonry, the influence or not of the Templars, the curiosities in some higher degrees or the contribution made by some eminent Brother.

I have to declare at once that the lectures presented in this collection are for the former group and have all been given, some of them many times, when lodges have no candidate, when they just want a change from perpetual ceremonies, or as part of a regularly thought-out plan of basic education for lodge members. Anyone can, by careful searching, find out anything that I have presented. The surprising thing is that most Masons just don't go searching and the result is very often that they say to me, 'I just didn't know that'. Therein lies the reason for this collection's title.

It ought to be added that, in this increasingly 'open' period of Freemasonry, I have had the inestimable privilege of speaking nearly 50 times to gatherings of Masons and their wives or friends, normally in their lodge rooms with the brethren in full regalia, but with the lodge proper closed or 'called off'. The lectures marked with an asterisk are those that have been given to such gatherings and have been found to meet a special need there as well as in closed lodges. I do have others for such occasions that are not included here.

I therefore commend these pages to my brethren who are now looking for new material to use without always asking a lecturer like myself to be in attendance. Any of these talks, because that is what they really are, are able to be used by anyone who so wishes, if a simple acknowledgement of their source is given when being delivered. If they are used with ladies present I will be the first to rejoice and also one who would love to hear what kind of reaction there is from the audience on such an occasion.

If the pages inform, encourage, entertain and extend the knowledge of our great Craft, I shall be fully rewarded for any effort involved.

V. Wor. Bro. the Rev. Neville Barker Cryer
York, 1998

The Origin of our Lodge Room

Familiar as most of us have become with gathering in our various meeting places it is easy to forget, and in some cases even to remember ever knowing, what were the locations from which our Masonic assemblies arose. There were at least three of these and it is about them that I want to talk to you for a little while tonight. Some of you will already know something of what I am going to mention but for the benefit of others present some of what I say may be quite new and thus of special interest.

The first source of our lodge room is an open yard which was used by working, or operative, Masons. Some lodge rooms, like those in Castlegate, York, Pocklington, Scarborough and Thirsk, actually portray this by having the ceiling painted blue like the dome of heaven and then putting stars there to show that it is meant to represent the open sky. What is more the arrangement of the stars, as at Pocklington, is meant to be exactly what you would observe were you to look at a clear sky on any lodge night.

Around the room are the signs of a workmen's yard. There are pieces of worked stone at different stages – a rough ashlar for the apprentice to work on (as they still do in Bristol lodge rooms), a smooth ashlar which was the masterpiece of the Fellow of the Craft, and an ashlar being lifted or lowered by a triangular metal derrick, or, as in York and again Scarborough, a wooden hoist, made for the same purpose. Here are clear indications of work in progress and the signs of how those who use this 'yard' gain advancement by the state of their 'workings'.

The names we give to the Masons who gather here are also reminiscent of that older time. They are Entered Apprentices (that means 'entered on the books'); Fellows of the Craft and Master Masons. They wear aprons which derive from the kind of clothing they first adopted – though how that came about is a matter for further talk. And we have here the same tools that were

9

used in the middle ages for the Craft (notice that word) of cutting out, stone carving and laying.

We have the mallet and chisel, the level and plumbline, the measure and square, and because the Masons depended on an architect/Master to draw designs and lay the whole ground plan of the building on which they were to work we see a skirret, pencil (once chalk), tassels and compasses. In all these ways we are thus constantly reminded of our original work place. Yet this was not all. Because the weather might be inclement and the workers want to lay off and have their 'noonday fast broken' so they had to have a place for their 'noon-jeune' ('le nuncheon' which became 'Luncheon'). Here may I remind you that when people began to eat more, and before their work began, they moved the name of that later meal to the earlier hour and called it 'break-fast'. But to return to this yard.

Where did they work in the dry and eat apart? In a 'lean-to' that was built against the wall of the church, castle or Cathedral they were building. The mediaeval word for that was 'allogement' and it was from this that the English word 'lodge' derives. Steadily the lodge was made more stable and secure with firm walls and a door to shut, and with tiles to cover it. It was in that room that private meetings of the Masons were held and that is what we do to this day. Freemasons meet privately, not secretly, in a lodge in the yard and a 'tiler' keeps it secure.

And just one more thing – do you see the implement carried by someone – a trowel? Anyone who lays bricks or stones knows how important that tool is. What you may not know is that in one 18th century tradition the trowel was worn by the brother who kept the inner door of the lodge as the ostensible preserver of the lodge's privacy. We have kept it because it reminds us that this tool helps us to bind things together and hence symbolises our being bound by our obligation to, but also in charity with, one another. That is why the Grand Lodge eventually drew on its store of tradition and assigned it as what the 'Charity Steward' should wear today.

This room also derived from the meeting place of a Guild. It is from the guild that we get most of our officers' names, W.M., Wardens, Deacons, Scribe or Secretary, Treasurer, Almoner and above all the Chaplain. You can also see items round the room that Guildsmen would have recognised at once. These are the Banner (which they always used when processing outside on their feastday), the almsbox (for they emphasised charity and self-help was a high priority), the ballot-box (which they used for making important decisions discretely, and most of all in selecting new members), the candlesticks (for that was how their meeting places were lit), the wands (for remember that they took the name 'warden' from their parish churches and there the Wardens still have their rods or wands) and the wands here in the lodge were first held by the wardens and only later transferred to their deacons when these became necessary officers after the Union of 1813. Not least there was the Bible. This important item, which only replaced the book of the Latin Gospels after 1550, was, with their Chaplain, to remind the Guildsmen that they were ultimately in the presence, and acting with the guidance, of God.

Notice here, however, that what we do in a lodge room today is to combine the old yard and the Guildhall by putting the square and compasses on top of the open Bible whenever the lodge room is used for a Masonic meeting. No lodge in the English Constitution can ever be held without these three items set out like that. I am sure that you know that they represent the Word (the V. S. L.) of the Great Architect (the square) of the Universe (the compasses). If there are any who wonder what it is that we get up to in our meetings let them at least know that we consciously intend to meet in the presence of God and of his Holy Word.

It is at this point that we have to remember something else about the Guilds in this country. In all the largest cities of the 14th to 17th centuries there were annual processions in which the Guilds took part and in which they sometimes performed, and sometimes paid others to perform for them, plays of a sacred nature. It should therefore come as no surprise to learn that in this room we too perform 'ritual plays'. Some of them, indeed, are directly linked to themes in the old plays produced by the Guilds of Masons. To enter into further explanation here would require another lecture but I assure you it was so (and any Masons interested may care to consult my Prestonian Lecture for 1974 on 'Medieval Drama and the Craft').

It only remains to account for the third origin of our lodge meeting place. This is no less than the Temple of Solomon. To explain this in full would again take much longer than we have time for this evening but let me point out four things that suggest that this is so. The first thing is the mosaic flooring. At first sight this may not seem to be very remarkable but the more you learn about this form of covering the more fascinating it becomes. What is most interesting is how this sort of decoration – black and white squares – became the norm for our rooms. Why, for example, are chapel floors as far apart as those in the castles of Durham and Malaga in Southern Spain of just this kind?

The answer lies in a tradition which was behind the pictures that we still possess in the earliest printed and illustrated Bibles of the 16th century. Here all the woodcuts and engravings show the floor of the Temple **or** Solomon's palace as black and white squared. Of course there were no coloured pictures then so that was thought to be the original plan and design for the house of God and the great king's dwelling. When the first drawings or cloths used in the lodges at taverns and inns came into use they revealed the same chequered flooring as part of the 'Temple'. Since these lodges never had permanent rooms they could not have carpets but when, by the early 19th century, Masons began to have more fixed meeting places, and eventually their own premises, they had these carpets made of the same design. This carpet or floorcovering is therefore a representation of the floor of Solomon's Temple or house.

That is why, when a lodge starts its life, it is consecrated, and the heart of that ceremony takes place at the centre of such a carpet. It is for this reason that we call the lodge a 'holy place' where no food is eaten, no smoking happens and no drink is consumed. It is called 'Mosaic' because the Temple design was derived from the Tabernacle in the wilderness made by Moses and his associates, Aholiab and Bezaleel, and because, not surprisingly, the earliest pictures of that structure also show a tent with black and white carpets. 'Mosaic' in this context does not refer to marble floor work – it has the sense of 'sacred'.

The second sign is that we have, in the East of this room, for all Speculative Masonic lodge rooms are orientated like churches, a main chair or Throne that is called by us 'the throne of Solomon'. Here sits the Master of the Lodge and in a real sense we expect him to be just and wise like the one whose chair he occupies. He has also to remember ritual like that King and to be able to deliver it with dignity and meaning. Yet that is not all. In front of this throne is at least one pedestal, and in most Northern lodges there are two. The one on which the candidates take their obligations is often called, and in America

and Canada always called, an 'altar'. In the latter countries it also always stands, like the same feature in Ireland and Bristol, at the centre of the floor. This again points out the nature of the building as a 'Temple' where prayer is offered. In Scotland a bowl of incense or other aromatic substance is sometimes placed on the top of the altar and this even more underlines the place as one in which sacred rites take place. There are actually some 'altars' in English lodge rooms where there is an indentation in the top of the altar and the members of the lodge possessing these are often puzzled as to why this should be so. It simply relates to a previous, similar use.

The third feature which reminds us that we are in the representation of the Temple is the presence of the two great pillars. Once they always stood, or were first of all drawn, at the west of the space where the lodge met but whilst they retain this position, as in Bristol or at two halls in York as in several West Yorkshire 'Temples', they are nowadays mostly often relegated to the Warden's pedestals and called 'columns'. The columns are more correctly those that support the candles beside the pedestals and these, of course, once stood in the middle of the room *around the altar* as they still do in the next major stage of Masonry beyond the Third Degree. The columns belong to the portico of King Solomon's Temple and these are therefore seen on the first Tracing Board. So when we have opened a Lodge the Temple is symbolically present there also.

The last feature of this Solomon connection is found on the warrant that permits this lodge to meet. It is a seal that is affixed to every such document and it bears certain symbols, one of which is the Ark of the Covenant that once stood in the Holy of Holies. You may know, and if you did not then believe me when I tell you, that this latter chamber was in the extreme **West** of the Temple and was a totally dark space that was rarely visited. This fact is not always brought to our notice when we inspect our warrant or the certificates of membership which each Mason possesses. So important was this connection for early lodges that to this day the oldest lodges in Lewes, Sussex, and Taunton, Somerset, have a model Ark in the centre of the floor whenever the Lodge is opened.

We are those who are not ashamed to act as the descendants of those who revered the Temple and the Ark. Here in such a room as this we strive to carry out activities that relate to that Holy Place and that is why, around the Ark, are certain ancient Hebrew characters that spell – Kodesh l'Adonai – Holiness to the Lord. That is the most important thing to remember about every Masonic meeting room and every Freemason: it and he is meant to be dedicated in 'Holiness to the Lord': that is really why we meet **here**.

A Walk round your Lodge Room

We begin our journey round the lodge room by explaining the reason why the principal officers are seated where they are. Perhaps the fact that they are in the East, west and South is such a normal thing for us to see that it may be something of a surprise to learn not only that this was not how operative Masons always met but that even today there are lodges, e.g. at places as far apart as Stamford and Edinburgh, as well as when we go to dine, where our usual positions in the lodge room are not normal at all. Let me explain.

Original Masonic symbolism required that the Master of the lodge should be at the apex of any triangle of officers when a meeting was convened. This meant that he was either at the corner of a **square** or at the apex of a pair of **compasses**. Accordingly, the Master either had the Junior Warden on his extreme left and the Senior Warden immediately opposite – thus forming the shape of a square: or he had the Senior and Junior Wardens at the two farthest corners of the space in front of him, thus representing the positions formed by a pair of compasses.

Moreover, the Masons met, and ate, at tables in the middle of the room and, since the Masons assembled symbolically in the Temple of Solomon, with the two great pillars at the entrance to the lodge (or Temple), the Master was seated with the J.W. at the end of the left sprig and the S.W. at the end of the one in front, or alternatively, with a table for the Master and past Masters and one sprig opposite them with the two wardens facing each other at its foot.

There was also another major difference. The Master sat in the West, and the Wardens thus sat, in the first arrangement, in the North and East, whilst in the second arrangement the Wardens were in the North-East and the South-East. In this latter case the Wardens actually sat beside or in front of the pillars. That this form of seating for the principal officers was the case is revealed by some ritual that we still observe: for when the W.M. asks the Junior Warden why he is placed where he is, he replies, "To **mark** the sun at its meridian . . ." If he was in the North or North-East, that is exactly what he would be able to do . . . to 'mark', notice or remark on the noonday position of the sun and thus be able to call the brethren from labour to refreshment. Today we have changed the meaning of the term and it now suggests that we '**represent** the sun'. That is not what the ritual says or means. And exactly the same is true when we come to the Senior Warden. He 'marks' the setting sun from the East or South East and knows it is time to call an end to the proceedings. I have even found two lodges where even today the W.M. says, 'to Mark, or See, the rising sun'.

All this was altered when the Premier Grand Lodge created its own new rules and ritual after 1717. The Master was now expected to sit in the East 'since all churches and places of worship are so oriented', though quite why the W.M. should sit where the altar of such places of worship then normally stood with the minister facing East is another whole subject for debate that we cannot enter into here.

As the number and importance of Past Masters grew, so the top table extended and you had the W.M. at the centre, the senior Masons flanking him and the Secretary and Treasurer occupying the two ends of that sprig, North and South. You still see those officers there in the West and North of England, though not in the South and South-East. When the Master left the floor and went East the J.W. remained as before. I hope that you can now see how the present form of seating began to emerge.

After the Act of Union of the Grand Lodges of 1813, some noticeable changes followed. The form of arranging the Lodge used by one lot of Masons was recommended for the work in the lodge room and this had the W.M. and Wardens in the East, West and South, but as a form of compromise, the old alternative 'compass' form of placing the principal officers was adopted for the after proceedings at table.

The other great change was that the idea of combining the eating of a meal and the performing of a ceremony in one room at the same time was no longer permitted. Either the ceremony must be performed and the signs of it removed before the tables for dining were brought in or the members were encouraged to move to another room altogether for their meal. Food, drink, clay-pipes and even spittoons were forbidden during the lodge meeting and yet so persistent was the connection that in 1852, forty years after the Union, the lodge at Ludlow recorded that a large bowl of punch was still carried into the lodge-room after the ceremony of installing the new Master. When this was reported to the P.G.M., the Lodge was duly singled out for reprimand and they had henceforth to call the lodge off and retire – to another room for TEA.

The pedestals before these officers are also due to the same event. When the tables were ordered to be removed in 1813, the officers, including the Secretary and Treasurer, still needed

somewhere to place their gavels or papers, etc., so bits of the table were in effect retained. (Where appropriate a word has to be said about the separate or central 'altar' or pedestal for obligations.)

The pillars and globes now need our attention. These represented, as has been said, the entrance to the Temple. Initially, of

course, they were simply drawn on the floor of the lodge alongside or within the square of the table sprigs. When lodges began to have their own lodge rooms, they became objects and used to stand at the west end of the flooring as e.g. they still do in Bristol, Barnstaple or York. Candidates and members would enter the Craft and the lodge between them. Yet some lodges (or was it their DCs?) began to find them a nuisance and so they were removed, to the side as at Hartlepool, to just inside the door as in Halifax, outside the door as at Exeter or reduced in size and banished to the Wardens' pedestals. Not that the latter was altogether incorrect since we have seen that in ancient practice the Wardens were associated with these pillars. What is important to note is that albeit we now call these items 'Columns', they are in fact the modern replicas of the old 'Pillars'. The presence of the globes on the top of them shows what they are for the pillar 'Boaz' carried the terrestrial globe and the pillar of the S.W. carried the celestial one. If you want to know where the true columns are, then look at the candlesticks.

A word about the globes here may be in order. Any thinking Mason is bound to wonder why, if these pillars represent those which stood at the porchway or entrance to King Solomon's Temple they support these globes when it is manifest that in the time of Solomon there was no awareness of the world being round, even if the constellations of the heavens were familiar. How do we explain this? The answer is twofold.

The first reason is that in the description of these pillars in the Bible, we are told that on the top of them were objects called in Hebrew 'Gooloth'. The word means 'any kind of rounded vessel'. In the case of the Tabernacle in the wilderness or of the Temple in Jerusalem this meant that on the top of the pillars there were two bowls into which a form of inflammable oil was placed and the pillars therefore seemed to be constantly alight. They gave off smoke by day and a flame by night and that is the origin of the biblical description of them as creating a pillar of cloud by day and a pillar of fire by night. If you go to the Masonic Temples at Barnstaple or Bath to this day bowls are what you will see on top of the full size pillars that are used.

Yet the formers of our ritual were also influenced by the fresh knowledge that came to our land in the 16th century with the Renaissance. They began to see bibles with pictures and in the Geneva Bible of 1560 they saw the pillars of the Tabernacle and of the Temple at Jerusalem with circular balls covered with netting at the summit of those pillars. Since the circular nature of the Earth was also then discovered and in every gentleman's study two sets of globes began to be common, it was almost inevitable that a terrestrial and celestial globe should replace the old 'gooloth'. By the 18th century the present forms had come to stay. (An aside about the Services term – 'goolies'.)

Let us now consider the candlesticks. These were also not originally at the senior officers' places but were, at the Lodge Opening, placed in a triangular formation on the unrolled 'drawing', later board or carpet, in the centre of the ceremonial area. (Mention Pilgerloge, London and Olicana, Ilkley Los.) The reasons for their removal was the same as for the removal of the Pillars, the symbolic tools and objects or later tracing boards and in some cases, the altar. The DC or the Preceptor found these items an obstacle to doing the floorwork he wished. Hence in this case the candlesticks were 'sidelined' and since the form of using them

in the centre once involved the Principal officers where better to put them than at the Wardens' and Master's pedestals. It was Masonic regalia manufacturers who then helped to devise the 'Three Orders of Architecture' columns to hold them. In some old lodges there can be found a special array of the five 'columns' for instruction.

Mention of the candlesticks and other symbolic items on the floor of the lodge may be something new to you but if you were to visit the oldest lodges in Lewes, Sussex or Taunton, Somerset you would find that to this day they have, in the centre of the carpet, an array of items – the Ark of the Covenant, the two tablets of the Ten Commandments, a pot of incense, the Master's tile, the tripod with a pulley, the two globes and the tools of the appropriate degree. Where did this idea come from. Well, let me take you back to the tables at which the early 18th century Masons sat. I said then that in the angle of the square tables or along one side of the T-shaped tables a drawing of certain items would be prepared on the floor for the candidate both to see and to pass over. When lodges eventually had their own meeting places some lodges transferred that drawing to a permanent cloth or board whilst other lodges produced the actual objects. Incidentally this is probably why, in many lodges in the South of England, the DC orders the tracing board to be put in the centre of the room for the whole of the ceremony.

This leads naturally to why some lodges still square the lodge room. When the candidate was introduced he was not at first allowed to cross the floor on which this drawing stood. He was taken round the outside of the tables and that is why to this day the first request made to the lodge officers for admission is by knocking on the right shoulder of the seated Wardens. Originally you approached them from the rear.

Accustomed as you may be to the position of other officers in your own lodge, you need to realise that these can vary a great deal. (This can be illustrated with the D.C., Secretary and Treasurer.)

The post of I.G. is also a result of the 1813 agreement and merits some attention. In the 18th century it was quite common for the newest apprentice Mason to be armed with a trowel or sword and placed at that post. If you doubt me then I have to remind you of some words of the 1° Charge: "Monarchs themselves have not thought . . . to exchange the sceptre for the **trowel**" – not, you notice, the gavel. Why ever do we say this? It is because it means that Kings and Rulers are not ashamed to descend from their exalted secular position to the lowest position in the lodge – holding a trowel as the newest initiate at the door of a Mason's lodge. That is of course why we say this in the First Degree charge.

Whilst we are talking about implements of office, a word must be said about wands. The D.C.'s wand was bestowed upon him by the W. M. who is charged with keeping order in the Lodge and in Keighley the clips for securing the W. M.'s wand are still on the pedestal. Similarly to what occurred with musical conductors, some lodge DCs now have a baton which has been reduced from the larger wand. Again, the Wardens, following Church practice, were also given wands of office, but they duly bestowed these on the Deacons when, after 1813, such officers were now required in each lodge. In Selby, Yorkshire, you can, however, still see the batons that were in the form of the original Wardens wands.

As a further proof of where the wands belong let me tell you that in certain very old lodges, such as Phoenix, Sunderland, Durham, the wands of the Deacons carry a sun and a crescent moon. This is because the one belonged to the Warden who 'marked' the midday sun and the other was that of the Warden who perceived the moon approaching. Later lodges adopted a sign of a messenger when the wands were placed in the hands of the moving Deacons and Hermes or Mercury was the figure that appeared. At or after the Union lodges adopted the dove that brought the message of hope and peace to Noah in the Ark but why that sign was chosen cannot here be gone into.

We must finally look at the tracing board and carpets that now adorn every English lodge though you may care to know that Irish lodges now do not have the former and neither do Scottish lodges necessarily have them. The boards began life as drawings made by the Tyler with chalk or charcoal on the wooden floor of the meeting room and these drawings were usually expunged (literally) after each meeting by the newest initiate. Not surprisingly the drawing could often be crude and even indecipherable. Some lodges therefore began to put the actual items on the floor (refer to Taunton above) but others began to have a black and white line drawing (see Haworth, Yorkshire) or a coloured drawing on a cloth or board that could be kept permanently and yet removed after meetings. From these cloths or boards which each lodge devised more standard ones developed as the number of lodges grew. There are three interesting things about them as they developed:

1. Some lodges have composite boards (Cheltenham and Greenock);
2. Some lodges have their boards on permanent open display, (York);
3. Some Lodges have boards with items no longer explained, (Derby).

Finally, the carpet. In another talk which I deliver I explain why the carpet has special significance for us who meet in a 'Temple' and also why it has this distinctive chequered design. On every known tracing board there is a Mosaic or chequered flooring, and in some lodges the base of the candlesticks also displays this same design. As I told you that the Lodge once met on the floor so it is on the carpet that every new lodge is consecrated and in a very real sense the bounds of the carpet are really the limits of the lodge proper. That is why you will often see tassels at the four corners of the carpet: they symbolise where the original shape of the site for the building was marked out by skirret lines which were then tied at the corners. Because today we think of the whole room being the limits of the lodge in some halls (e.g. as at Pickering) the tassels are actually hung up in the corners of the roof.

Such, Brethren (and friends), is some explanation of what we see around us. I trust that you will the more appreciate the significance of what is used and the history that has produced it.

Where did we get our clothing?

The style of clothing associated with the Craft of Freemasonry has a very ancient ancestry. For those in the North of England it may appropriately be related to the garb adopted by the building tradesmen of the Roman legions who were assigned to creating and then guarding the structures such as Hadrian's and Antonine's Walls between the Scots and the citizens of Britannia. Out on that breezy, not to mention wet and chilly, employment those 'Masons' would have been delighted to be able to use the skins and wool of the sheep killed for food and fix those hides around their bodies – with the wool against their skin in winter and in reverse during the better weather.

The whole skin, with the remnants of the skin on the legs useful for tying the garment round the back, would thus have protected the chest and lower abdomen when carrying out work in smoothing, shaping or laying stone blocks or ashlars. It was a most efficient garment. It was to remain virtually unchanged in design, albeit the fabrics might vary, throughout the whole of history of the operative Mason's craft.

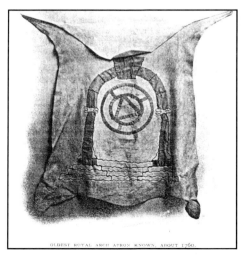

OLDEST ROYAL ARCH APRON KNOWN, ABOUT 1760.

Indeed, so established had it become as a token of the 'Mason's art' that when our form of speculative Masonry was established it was still this kind of extended apron which was taken as the style to be continued albeit thongs, rather than skin remnants, might secure the garment round the body. (Point out the oldest Royal Arch apron of mid 18th century provenance with these features.)

The 18th century Speculatives began to trim the length but not the shape and only in the late 18th century was the apron halved (except for Apprentices) and buttoned to determine the separate degrees. The Apprentice still had his upper half erect as one requiring the greatest protection from possible accidents with stone and implements and that it why, to this day, there are some of our lodges which insist that the Entered Apprentices should keep the flap of their more modest aprons erect until they are passed to the next degree. What also developed was the practice of turning up the left bottom corner of the apron to signify that the Mason was a F.C. and then both bottom corners to show that the brother was a full Master Mason who had a ready made pocket for his essential tools. In North America this latter practice is still widely maintained.

It was as the 18th century progressed that the vanity of Masons also developed. Whereas the original intention was that the working Mason would be satisfied with a skin of some sort, whether of a sheep or cow, the emerging gentleman Mason wanted something of a more genteel fashion. The arrival of cotton, cashmere, satin, silk or even velvet meant that by the latter quarter of the 18th century the variety of stuffs used for the adornment of Masons grew and the social status of a brother might begin to be discerned not only by the material used for the base of the apron, but also by the quality of needlework that decorated its surface.

It has to be recalled that at exactly this same period, the number of available Masonic degrees increased considerably and the status of a Mason could now be designated not only by the sumptuousness or simplicity of the stuff used but by the designs of other degrees which might be symbolically illustrated on both the flap and the front of the apron. (Some examples of the variety that developed should now be demonstrated either by illustrations or with actual items.)

By the early years of the 19th century, there began to appear a great range of private aprons, some of which would display steps in Freemasonry that were quite unknown to other Masons who had less decorated clothing. There was even a danger, if not an actual possibility, of creating divisions between brethren once more by reason of this flaunting of variegated regalia. It can be appreciated, of course, that the display of more and more degrees by the greater number of symbols portrayed was both an effective advertisement and a direct inducement to draw brethren 'beyond the Craft'.

Yet there was, at just this period, an event in English Freemasonry that was to affect Masonic clothing up to the present day. As I have explained in another lecture elsewhere, this event was the Union of the two major opposing Grand Lodges that had emerged in the preceding century. This Union, very largely under the direction and influence of the Duke of Sussex for the next thirty years, was to make significant changes in the management and appearance of the Craft, and not least in the matter of what Freemasons should wear.

What happened in the decade following the establishment of this Union in 1813 was that first a decision was taken that there should be specified, uniform patterns for the type of aprons that were to be worn by different kinds of brethren. These patterns developed by trial and error but they were from the start ruled by three fundamental principles:

1. they were to be standard for the ranks indicated and no variations were to be allowed;
2. the basic material was to be the original skin of a lamb and other more fancy materials were excluded;
3. each degree in Freemasonry was to be provided with its own form of apron and those who had progressed in the Craft or

beyond it were not allowed to adorn their aprons with symbols not fitting for the grade of Masonry in which brethren were assembled.

With these principles to guide their deliberations, the new United Grand Lodge was able to achieve two particular objectives. They could on the one hand establish a new kind of control on the Craft which would no longer represent that of the Grand Lodges that had ruled previously. On the other they could balance their new insistence on admitting any free man of whatever political, religious, racial or social background by showing that it was no longer possible to have a division of dress. Everyone, from the Grand Master to the simple Entered Apprentice, was to wear the statutory clothing for his position and the flamboyant dress of the earlier age was to be for ever consigned to cupboards or collections in museums.

It should be said that this was not the first time that there had been such an attempt at the regulation of Masonic dress, for the Premier Grand Lodge in the 18th century had already ruled that Grand Officers were to wear the royal or Tyrian blue of the reigning Hanoverian dynasty whereas the Officers of the Grand Lodge of Scotland to this day wear the green of the Stuart royal House. It can be well imagined that in view of the Jacobite, or Stuart, uprisings that troubled Britain between 1715 and 1745, any possibility of green being applied in England would have seemed downright treasonable.

At the same time the Grand Lodge had decreed on crimson as the colour of the aprons worn by what was known as the Grand Stewards Lodge and it is precisely because this was established so early and had so long a pedigree that all subsequent Stewards, even in some private lodges like the Royal Cumberland, No. 44 in Bath, adopted crimson as the colour of this office. (One could here show a Prov. Steward's apron.)

One feature of the newly designed aprons after 1813 was that they were to have no tassels or pendants. This was probably to sharpen up the appearance at a time when other means of attaching the apron by a belt and catch had overtaken the older method of using a cord that tied under the flap. The design was not persisted with save for one striking exception. To this day those who are appointed active Grand Officers and are provided with ceremonial dress when they are on duty will find that their aprons have no tassels. The aprons that they wear when attending lodges in a private capacity are just like those of other Grand Officers, with tassels, but to distinguish them when on duty for Grand Lodge, they continue to sport the original post-1813 design.

For the remainder of the troops, a number of slight variations were tried, but by about 1825 the forms of apron that you see about you today were at last determined. Let me explain some of their features so that we shall see how the old operative's garb has developed.

You will notice that the apron has been considerably reduced in size for the majority of brethren. It thus became much more easy to carry about when it now also became common for all Masons to have their own personal dress. That not everyone had their own aprons hitherto is revealed by two facts of current ceremonial practice. One is that during the progress of a candidate from his admission to becoming a Fellow of the Craft, he is today provided by the lodge with two aprons to wear. It is only when he becomes a M.M. that he begins to have his own personal item. Yet in North America, it is still very often the custom that simple white aprons are provided in the lodge ante-room for any brethren attending, whether as members or visitors. Even the lodge officers, who have rather more decorative aprons during their term of service, are provided with these by the lodge. The brethren here started that practice in the 18th century when they took Masonry from these shores and thus they preserve for us something with which we are no longer familiar. Having our own personal aprons is now regarded as essential, but it was not always the case.

The simple white lambskin apron is still the dress in England for the Entered Apprentice, but when he moves on to become a Fellow of the Craft he finds that two rosettes have been attached. These rosettes are the formalised remnants of the buttonholes of which I spoke earlier as enabling the apron to be turned up to indicate the grade of the brother concerned and when we come to the still more elaborate apron of the Master Mason which the vast majority of Masons wear, we then find that the old buttonhole that enabled the Entered Apprentice's flap to be held erect has mysteriously re-appeared. One suspects that the number of rosettes now had a subtle reference to the fact that 2 meant the 2° and 3 meant the 3°. Their real purpose you now know.

When a Master Mason became a true 'Master' who ruled his lodge, his apron changed from having rosettes to having what many still call 'taus' but are really 'levels'. When you consider that to become a ruling Master you must have been a Warden and a Fellow Craft it is very appropriate that the new Master should wear the triple sign of having passed those essential offices.

You will notice that the Apprentice and F.C. aprons are attached round the body by the older method of cords or string whilst the M.M. and Installed Master's aprons are attached by a belt and a catch. To preserve the traditional mode of dress with the cords fastened at the front and under the flap with ends sticking out, the present form of tassels was devised. They have no symbolic significance whatsoever save that they remind us of our oldest operative aprons. The brethren may even be surprised to know that there are some aprons that have 9 or even 12 pendants so attempts at symbolising 7 prove pointless. To emphasise the status of a M.M. or ruling Master, the apron also acquired a light blue band around the whole of the exposed edges. It was light blue to distinguish it from the shade worn by Grand Officers. You may be interested to know that earlier there had once been a suggestion that the ruling Master's apron might be orange but as that was the colour of the Dutch royal House, it too was disallowed.

The apron, as you perceive, is worn in England over the jacket, but in Irish and Scots Masonry, it is worn beneath. This is because they contend that working Masons take off their jackets before putting on their aprons and that should still be the tradition we retain. The fact that they are now speculative Masons and put their jackets back on as gentlemen may seem 'Irish to us', but that at least is why they dress differently.

You will of course notice that besides the Grand Officers' clothing and that which I have just described, there is yet another variation in this lodge room. I refer to the Provincial or District clothing. (Here request one of such officers to stand and show his regalia.)

Though there had been Provincial Grand Lodges created in some areas long before 1813, it was only after that date that a distinctive form of clothing was created as a sort of half way house between the private lodges and the Grand Lodge. This was of course part of a plan to enhance the status of the Provincial administrations which were becoming more and more necessary as the number of lodges increased quite significantly in the 19th century.

Accordingly, you will note that the Provincial Officers have aprons which show the dark blue of the Grand Lodge but with a permanent fringe of gold braid that is not present on the Grand Lodge undress. Moreover the apron always bears a roundlet on its face with the name and symbol of office that pertains to that Province. For Grand Officers there is a symbol but no wording whatsoever. This clothing is first worn when a brother attends the Provincial Grand Lodge at which his new rank is announced and confirmed.

You may perhaps by now have wondered when I am going to mention the matter of collars. The time is now because this is a topic with its own history and variations. If you want to see how the collar took its rise the best place to visit is the Tapton

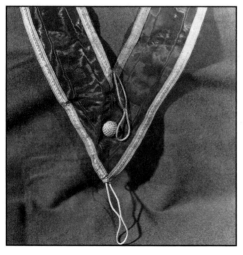

Masonic Hall, Sheffield. There, in a series of remarkable portraits of long past Grand Officers you will see that in order to append their office jewels, they first attached them to a single strand of blue silk and hung them round their necks. As the 18th century progressed these strands became steadily broader and as they did they had to be strengthened to lie flat. As they became broader, they could not pass through the eyelet at the top of the jewel so another piece of cord was attached to the base of the wide ribbon, fed through the eyelet and then looped over the ribbon and attached to a button or knob above the base. When eventually the ribbon became large material and tailored collars with a clip sewn into the end to hold the jewel the old cord and knob were symbolically retained. The knob, let me emphasise, is not a miniature beehive.

The idea of more formal and even silver-decorated collars for the ruling Master of a Lodge came in the 19th century as a direct copy of the collars worn by Mayors or the Masters of Guild companies. They may be part of Lodge tradition but they have no Masonic significance at all. As with several of our Lodge pieces of furniture it has played directly into the hands of the Masonic regalia manufacturers and given them still more cause to rejoice at the vanity of humankind.

It was precisely this factor of the desire for more decoration that led in the 19th century to three other sets of appendages. To introduce the first let me explain why most Masons wear gloves though I hasten to add that there are still some English Lodges, like my own mother one, Tyrian 253, where gloves have never been worn in over 200 years.

The operative Mason did not wear gloves to do his work as they would have hindered his delicate use of tools. The person who wore hat and gloves and carried a staff was the Architect-Master Mason who drew designs, planned schemes and governed his brethren. One can only assume that when the partial degree of being a Master-Mason came into being it was thought that wearing gloves was a perk that could now be enjoyed. Wearing gloves, of course, was also a social practice for gentlemen in the 19th century when the idea of dark clothing or even dinner jackets came into fashion for lodge meetings. Anyone who has notions of 'innocence' and those attending funerals might ask themselves whether we are always at funerals and why we all do what only F.C.s did then.

The first extra appendage came about when not even gloves were thought to be sufficient to grace the offices of Master and

Wardens and to the gloves cuffs were attached to make gauntlets. There are, believe it or not, some of these glove-cum-gauntlets still seen around in lodge museums but since they were difficult to clean or repair the idea soon took on (again via Toye, Kenning or Spencer, once all separate) of having ordinary gloves and cuffs. That is why they appear now with the principal officers. Up to 25 years ago they had also become common for the Grand and Provincial officers but even during my lifetime they have lapsed in that regard and it is only in private lodges that they have been retained. They again have no Masonic lineage.

The next adornment was of collarettes. Just as I have explained that the formal jewels of Grand Officers began to be worn with ribbons round the neck and became collars so now it was felt that in addition to the collar, there might also be other decorations like those worn by honoured secular recipients of the MBE, OBE, K.B., K.C.B. etc. Thus arose the idea of a separate collarette for the ruling Master, one for past Provincial rulers, or for those rulers whose lodges had given towards the building of the present headquarters of Grand Lodge. Even the Prestonian Lecturer, the only official lecturer recognised by the Grand Lodge, was given a collarette that he wears for his lifetime.

And all this leads us finally to the matter of breast jewels. The idea of decorating someone for gallantry or outstanding service is again an idea that grew in the 19th century and led to those chests full of jewels that reached their dreadful apotheosis in the picture of the Nazi General, Goering. Sadly the same tendency developed in Freemasonry and from a period when one or two beautiful jewels might adorn the breast of an 18th century Mason the 19th and early 20th century Masons began to compete with each other as to who could 'rattle' the most. An example of how bad the matter could become is revealed in the picture of such a brother as is now shown. Fortunately steps have now been taken by Grand Lodge to restrict the number of jewels that a Grand

Officer can wear to two at the most. Other brethren are beginning to copy that example and the days of the ridiculously over-laden jewel-seeker are probably over. Just as Grand Lodge removed the over-bespangled aprons so now the tinkling Mason is a thing of the past. What is good is that our clothing is still mainly what it once was – an apron of lambskin denoting a hardworking brother.

Why do we say and do that?
(Some reflections on overlooked parts of the First Degree)

One of the distinctive features about Freemasonry is the fact that at its core is the constant repetition of certain fixed ceremonies. Becoming a Freemason requires a willingness not only to undergo those ceremonies oneself but to witness others taking those same ceremonies year in, year out. Even if we omit the visits that we may make with friends to their lodges one can in a normal lifetime witness the same actions and hear the **same words** (well, almost) up to a hundred times for each ceremony. Even for a keen Mason that is quite a lot to expect and for myself the only way to both bear and appreciate this constant repetition has been to try and listen to each ceremony in a spirit of fresh enquiry, asking myself, "Why do we say and do that?" or, if I am visiting another lodge, "Why do they say and do something slightly different?" It is in order to start some of our newer brethren on this path that I have chosen this idea for a talk tonight. I hope that it may help us all as we continue to witness our Craft ceremonies, including the Installation of a new Worshipful Master. So let us turn to the First Degree.

We begin with part of the W.M's interrogation of a candidate when he has first been admitted to the lodge room. "I demand of you, are you a free man and of the full age of 21 years?" These words, taken at their face value, must nowadays seem so obvious as almost to be worth omitting but they do in fact tell us two important things about the history of the organisation that we are about to join. First of all it shows that part of our Craft history dates back to a time when not all men in our land **were free**. That puts the institution back at least 400 years when it was understood that in order to gain admittance both to a Guild, and the apprenticeships that it controlled, an oath of obedience or allegiance had to be taken and such an act was impossible unless you were 'free' to do so. If you were already in bonds to another lord or master, then you could not do what was now required. The phrase 'are you a free man' therefore links us at once with medieval Masonic practice.

On the other hand, the phrase 'and of the full age of 21 years', whilst it seems perfectly reasonable to us, would have been unthinkable for a medieval apprentice. Such a candidate for Masonic work had to complete 7 years of learning under an acknowledged 'Master Mason' and it was at the age of 14 or 15 that such an apprenticeship would begin. The mention of 21 years thus tells us that the form of Masonry into which we are now to enter derives from a much later period which was that age when Speculative Freemasonry was taking its new form under the Premier Grand Lodge after 1717. So contained within this easily dismissed query of the Worshipful Master we have the beginnings of Masonic history of our present Order. It is one that derives some of its parts from its medieval past, but is distinct from that past by creating new rules for non-operative Apprentices. They now had to be above what was in the 18th and 19th centuries the legal age for undertaking oaths and declaring obligations.

The candidate duly takes the obligation of an Apprentice Freemason and is then commended to the assembled brethren as "a fit and proper person to be made a Mason". Again, this latter phrase slips off our tongues without a moment's thought. If the candidate has been vetted by the Lodge Committee, voted on by ballot of the members and has now willingly paid the fees and revealed his submission to the Supreme Being of his life, what else can he be but a 'fit and proper person' to be accepted? He is, we would thus think, socially and personally acceptable and thus a 'fit and proper person'. But that is not what it was meant to mean originally.

As we saw in our last reflection, the words we use in our ceremonies often recall earlier operative practice and it is to such a period that these words now direct us. To be an apprentice at all, a candidate had to be acceptable as a physically satisfactory human being. He had have all his limbs and all his senses. He had in fact to be able to see, to feel, to hear, to taste or speak and to smell. That is what it meant 'to be a fit person' for apprenticeship. And that, for candidates up to the late 18th century **and in** Speculative Freemasonry, was part of what actually took place. He was asked to read something, he was then blindfolded and asked to distinguish a knock, a bowl of incense, and a sharp pointed instrument. He thus established that his nose, mouth and touch were all normal. We may note that apart from the bowl of incense, which is still used in some Scottish lodges, all the tests are **still present** and have been undergone before the W.M. thus declares this person 'a fit' subject for acceptance by the lodge. Even so, he had also to be able to proceed round the lodge, to show the use of his limbs.

As to whether the candidate is a 'proper' one, a writer on medieval practice says this, "Apprentices are not to tell tales or repeat the gossip of their master or fellows . . . and of more particular interest is a section enjoining courteous behaviour when all are dining together 'yn chambur', which we may reasonably interpret as in the lodge." (Salzman p.41). Being a 'fit and proper' person, when it is thus explained, takes on a whole new set of allusions.

Have you also wondered why, when being taken round the lodge room the first time, the candidate is made to strike the Wardens on the right shoulder? The answer is simple but revealing. In the original ceremony of admission the candidate was not allowed to walk 'in the lodge' until he had been correctly admitted to the fraternity. He walked round the outside of the assembled lodge tables and thus approached the Junior Warden from the rear. To attract his attention he thus struck him on the shoulder nearest to him at which the Warden rose, turned to the right and addressed the newcomer.

Having been permitted to enter this 'Junior' gate with the password of 'Free and of good report', the candidate still has to stay on the outside and repeat the same procedure from the back of the Senior Warden. It is only when these two gates are passed that the Master is requested to receive the candidate and that is why the Deacon is now to instruct the candidate in the required approach steps **within** the lodge and **across** the carpet. I find it fascinating that even in lodges which are very strict about squaring the lodge they still allow these steps and others to be taken on the carpet or central floor of the lodge room. That shows that the candidate is now actually entering the lodge. Moreover, the fact that the candidate has passed the Warden's gates means that he has also passed the two great pillars at the entrance of King Solomon's Temple copies of which are on the Wardens' pedestals.

The steps he now takes, however, are to be symbolically hesitant and uncertain. That is why several ways of approaching the pedestal are allowed. All of them avoid square and regular steps because we are shortly to be told that all such forms are 'true and proper signs to know a Mason by' and the candidate is not yet a Mason. There is therefore no one fixed form of approach and the one used in this lodge is simply to make conducting the ceremony easier and so that the Deacon will have words that he can learn to say. Many rituals require the steps to be irregular by making each step longer than the one before but no one can dictate how much longer each should be. The candidate is therefore no doubt confused, as he should be. What he has soon to learn is that he will then be given *regular* steps which he is to use in future.

It is when he has been entrusted with the traditional step, token and word that he is presented once more to the Wardens. They, having tested him in what he has been given, say 'Pass Boaz'. What exactly does that mean and where does the phrase come from?

To understand it fully, we have to know that the lay-out of operative lodges changed for different grades. In this respect the lodges owing allegiance to the Premier Grand Lodge adopted an earlier form with the W.M. at one end of the lodge room and the Wardens at the other, the latter placed about six feet or so apart. Each of the Wardens actually sat at the foot of one of the two pillars that stood at the entrance end of the room. In one sense they guarded, and in another sense they represented, the two great pillars that had adorned the entrance porch of the Temple of Solomon. Because the pillars looked out toward the entrance of the lodge room that on the left was called Boaz and it was here that the Junior Warden took his place. When the newly obligated and entrusted brother thus came to prove himself he was in fact standing before the pillar, Boaz, and in order to advance further he had to pass it. To do so, he was required to give the Warden that guarded it the proofs of his being a duly trusted brother. When he had done that the Warden could rightly say, "Pass Boaz" and the candidate could proceed. He knew what he was passing. Today, he still 'passes Boaz' because, as has already been mentioned, the pillar is now the miniature one that lies on the Junior Warden's pedestal. That is why, when the Warden gives the words he should carry the new brother's hand past the pillar with the globe on it so that he will indeed 'Pass Boaz'. Why I speak of 'pillars' and not columns is because that is what they are. The columns are the items at the sides of the Master and Wardens' pedestals which now carry candles and are of different orders of architecture.

The perceptive Mason may yet ask why, if the Wardens represent the two great pillars, the Senior Warden still says 'Pass Boaz' when he ought to say something else? The answer is because, as I also explain shortly, this First Degree ceremony was formed from the old Fellows degree and in that ceremony, both names were given as the candidate made his progress round the lodge. When this procedure was shared with the new Apprentice ceremony, only the first name could be used by both Wardens. Why also the seats of the Wardens are now in another arrangement than the one mentioned earlier cannot be explained here but might perhaps be something we can consider on another occasion.

Having passed the Wardens' pillars and been presented with his apron, the new Apprentice is placed in the North-East part of the lodge. Some lodges actually have, or place, a rough ashlar on the floor at this point and thus when the brother is told to stand with his left foot across the lodge and his right foot down it this is because not only has he so to stand to fit round the symbolic foundation stone but also because thus he stands upright in a regular square position – as he did for his obligation. As the North-East was the traditional area for foundation stones to be laid – because that is the part of any medieval church where the burial and resurrection of Christ were portrayed and He was then the foundation of belief and practice – so the newly Entered Apprentice is ever to recall that here is where he began his Masonic practice. As he is told, he begins to build on the foundation stone laid at this spot.

There is one other moment in the first degree ceremony when the candidate stands prominently before the brethren. It is when he is brought back, properly clothed, and receives an address given by the Junior Warden. It is an address full of meaning and time does not permit a proper consideration of it all. However, there is one sentence in its opening passage which is rarely or fully understood. The words are: "Monarchs themselves have not thought it derogatory to their dignity to exchange the sceptre for the trowel . . ." Since the sceptre is a symbol of rule and authority, shouldn't the word "gavel" be inserted here rather than the "trowel"? But no, the ritual formers knew what they were doing. In the 18th century, most lodges had a regular practice.

When a man was admitted as an Entered Apprentice, his first job was to guard the inner entrance of the lodge and in order to do that he was given a trowel as a symbol of secrecy and fraternal care. The phrase used in the 1° address now becomes meaningful. Even if a king or prince joins Masonry he was not unwilling to exchange his position of superiority over all other people in the realm for the lowest position in a Freemason's lodge. That is quite a lesson in humility which all need to emulate.

It is time however to close the lodge in which the brethren meet and where the ceremonies are performed. In this simple act of closure, however, there is one phrase that is again all too often spoken without much thought. It is, "having seen that all the brethren have had their due". What is that all about?

Most Masons today would, if pressed, say that it meant that we had got what we came for. If we expected an Initiation ceremony, that is what has been conducted and what was due to take place has happened. The real explanation behind this phrase is much more interesting but needs a little unpicking.

The operative ceremony of entering an Apprentice would not have had either an opening or a closing because these ceremonies were carried out for the main body of Fellows or Masters of the Craft and it was within their lodge that the introduction of apprentices would have taken place. However, the Premier Grand Lodge wanted to enhance the Initiation ceremony and so it took the original opening and closing of a Fellows Lodge and made it the basic opening and closing practice of all lodges. In doing so, however, it created an anomaly. The Apprentices were *not paid* for their work but instead were provided with housing and food by their Masters **who were** the paid Masons.

At the close of the Fellows of the Craft lodge the Senior Warden, who was responsible for seeing that the paid Masons received their 'due' wages, announced the fact to the Master. When this closing ceremony was transferred to a degree of Apprentices, the phrase was sometimes changed to 'the brethren have had their due'. But to this day there are many English lodges, especially in the North, who still say, 'having seen the wages paid as they are due' and to confirm the fact the Master further asks, 'And have all the wages been paid?' to which the Warden replies, 'They have, W.M., to the best of my knowledge and belief.' The traits of this still being a lodge with some operative history are thus not forgotten.

Such then are some of the features which we can so easily overlook as we both learn, recite or just hear our ancient ritual. That we are not just repeating words that have no real meaning will, I hope, have become all the clearer as we have looked more closely at some of the words we say. It might even be that in understanding them we will learn them all the more easily.

Neglected Aspects of the Three Degrees

At a time when it is probably true that the degrees of Freemasonry are performed more often and with as much care as has ever been the case, it may seem odd that anyone should dare to suggest that there is anything neglected in the three basic degrees of Craft Masonry. Yet what I am wanting to show and draw to our attention is not the fact that what we do is in itself neglected or mishandled. Rather that there are in our ceremonies, or ritual, parts that are nowadays either not fully explained or else passed over altogether and yet which, if adequately grasped, would add to and clarify the whole purpose of our Fraternity. Of course, I realise that what I may have to say can vary from country to country and you may want to inform me later that what I have focused on is very well explained and recognised in your particular working. If that is the case then may I assure you that such is not the case back in my own land and it will therefore have been both an education for you as to how others miss what you keep and how fortunate you are not to have such neglected aspects in your own Masonry. If, on the other hand, I am putting my fingers on neglected aspects of your own approach I hope this may be helpful and, in any case, these are only some of the areas I could highlight and you may care to go on and research others.

Let me begin with something that meets every English and Welsh Mason every time he enters his lodge room and yet which is very rarely, if ever, explained to him. I refer to the picture of a ladder that appears on the first degree tracing board and rises either vertically or diagonally across it. Its foot is usually resting on a pedestal bearing the V.S.L. and it ascends with rungs until its top disappears into a cloud or Shekinah above.

The ladder of course is more properly known as Jacob's ladder and in some 18th century tracing cloths or charts the figure of Jacob at its foot would have been shown.

The biblical story describes how, passing from Beersheba to Haran, Jacob stopped for the night. He took one of the stones from a nearby shrine and, using it as a pillow he lay down to sleep. In a dream he saw a ladder which rested on the ground but with its top reaching heaven and the angels of God going up and down on it. The Lord was standing beside him saying, 'I shall be with you to protect you wherever you go . . .' There is more but that will be enough.

It is because of this passage that the early ritual formers took the idea of the ladder and set it before us. Some of the ladders shown since the beginning of Masonry do indeed have angels ascending and descending upon them but there are other variations. One most frequently seen today shows three figures – the bottom one holding a cup, the middle one an anchor and the top one surrounded by 2 or 3 children. These respectively represent Faith, Hope and Charity and it is therefore no surprise to see one variation, indeed the one on the ceiling of the Grand Temple in London, where the symbols, without any figures, are a cross, a heart and a chalice. Yet again there are several boards where a finger points down to the V.S.L. on the pedestal and above the central anchor the ladder ends in a burst of golden light. The simplest variation appears in some Irish floorcloths where the plain letters F, H and C are shown.

Whilst there are these alterations to the characters on the ladder there is also endless variation in the number of staves or rungs that are shown. Some of the earliest have only three to suit the virtues displayed, some have nine, an Irish ritual declares that there should be eleven and some have fifteen to link up with the staircase in the next degree. Some have a much greater number and perhaps suggest that the total of the completed ladder should be nearer 72, which has its own special symbolism in other degrees. What is clear is that however the ladder is depicted it is obviously intended to be helpful and meaningful for the viewer. It is not there simply for decoration, but has a message to convey. This is in fact plainly stated in one of the lectures that used to be given following the First Degree but which is rarely, if ever, delivered in English lodges. The wording is significant.

"Describe the covering of a Masons' Lodge.

A Celestial canopy of diverse colours, even the Heavens.

As Masons, how do we hope to arrive at the summit?

By the assistance of a Ladder, called in Scripture Jacob's Ladder . . .

Of how many staves or rounds was this ladder composed?

Of **as many as comprise all the moral virtues**; three principal ones namely FAITH, HOPE and CHARITY.

Why these?

Faith in T.G.A.O.T.U., Hope in Salvation and Charity towards all men . . ."

And the Charge that completes this section of the Lecture is also worth quoting: "May every Mason attain the summit of his profession, where the just will most assuredly meet their reward."

This is, I trust, not simply a matter of words. We are here, at the very outset of our Masonic journey, brought face to face with the core of a vital conviction about who we are and how we are to see our lives. Moreover, it is all set within a context bounded by God's divine words on the one hand and his glorious omnipresence on the other – the two extremities of the ladder before us. Indeed, the very Lecture from which I quoted starts with these words:

"The nature, character, attributes and perfections of the Deity are faithfully delineated and forcibly portrayed, and are well calculated to influence our conduct towards Him, as our Father, Benefactor and Moral Governor, as well as in the proper discharge of the duties of social life." Those are powerful as well as beautiful sentiments.

Yet they are veiled from the ordinary Mason by their neglected use. What could be more effective than to indicate this ladder on the Tracing Board when certain words regarding our duty to God **are used regularly** by every Lodge in the Initiation of a Brother – "by imploring his aid on all your lawful undertakings and by *looking up to him* in every emergency for comfort and support?" In an age that makes so much use of visual aids, why do we neglect so potent and ancient a symbol?

It is time to turn from the ladder to the staircase of the second degree tracing board. Here, I dare say, I could expect a protest. How can you say that this feature is neglected in modern Freemasonry? Is it not true that very often in a Fellowcraft ceremony there is the presentation of the 2° Tracing Board and hence an explanation of the various steps that compose it?

That is indeed true but neglect can come in various forms. What I would ask here is what the ordinary Mason knows about the following?

Why do we have a curving staircase? Why do we have 15 or more steps? Why does the staircase on most boards today run upwards from South to West, whereas when we simulate the stairway in the ceremony we make it go from North to East? Why do we show the staircase as coming from a South facing doorway when all the evidence we have states that there was only one porchway or entrance and that at the East side of the Holy Place? Why do we say that the stairway led to the 'middle chamber' of the Temple when there often appears to be no lower or upper chamber? These are just a few of the questions that have always beset me since the first time that I heard the lecture delivered. There are others but time will even prevent me dealing

with more than just three of the ones above.

How many Masons are aware that in the 18th century the ritual in the North of England clearly stated that the Apprentices assembled in a lower chamber, the Fellowcrafts mounted to a middle chamber and the Masters ascended to an Upper Chamber? It was only in a ritual of 1802 that the present wording began to be used so that the peculiar singling out of the Fellowcrafts began and their place in a hierarchy determined.

Moreover, the fuller ritual mentioned above also made clear that these chambers were **on the outside** of the Holy Place and the higher ones were reached by stairs 'leading from the **South side'** of that sanctum.

It is when we know this (and I have brought you two pictures to show what I mean) that we can begin to understand the confusion that overtook Harris in the design of his 2° Board, so that though he drew the Holy Place in the upper part of his design, he created a South doorway in the Temple below and added the Pillars that belonged only to the main entrance. If, of course, you orientate the inner stairway to the middle chamber correctly then it enters the stairwell by a North entrance and makes its way upwards to the East. The answer to what we do in our lodges is explained.

Why we have 15 or more steps is revealed when you look back at one of the medieval cart plays that were performed in England for more than 250 years and in which productions the Operative

Masons had their part to play. One of their Patron Saints was the Virgin Mary and they knew her legends well, especially as some of them had to carve these for the churches they constructed.

In the stories connected with the childhood of Mary there is one that describes how 'the young innocent girl was brought to Jerusalem and there made the traditional entry of mounting **15 steps** towards the High Priest sitting on the throne of the **Inner Temple**, reciting on her way the appropriate 'Gradual' Psalms. Let us recall that Gradual came from **gradus** which meant grade or step or degree. In Coventry we still have the words used by her in those plays:

"The fyrst degre, gostly applyed,
It is holy desyre with God to be.
In trobyl to God I have cryed,
And in sped that lord hat herde me . . .
(The first degree charge??)
The secunde is stody, with meke inquyssyon veryly
How I shall have knowynge of Gods wylle . . .
(Do we recall what is the purpose of our 2°?)
The thrydde is gladness in minde in hope to be
That we shall be savyd all thus . . ."

Do you wonder any more about why it is '3, 5, 7 or more steps?'

Do you also understand why the staircase is curving, though in older floorcloths and boards it always twisted more, and from left to right and back again as in a spiral stairway. It was this latter kind of stair that the ritual formers had in mind for do they not say in the charge to the Fellowcraft, 'to extend your researches into the **hidden paths** of Nature and Science'? What better emblem of that search than to have the stairway of a lighthouse or tower in which every other step ahead is hidden from view and you have to mount to discover the whole truth. No longer the straight ladder of the 1° but a new way.

What I hope is now clear is that however often the normal lecture is given, vital additional information is withheld. Some of our essential instruction is wanting, and that is only answering three 2° questions.

Having arrived at the 2° it is time for us to look at the subject of ashlars. These have been important from the earliest days of Masonry, both Operative and Speculative, but when you see the objects lying inert and unmentioned in the lodge room one wonders what exactly they are meant to teach or convey. In English Masonry they are certainly neglected.

Let us begin with the words that are used at the North-East corner when a candidate is about to have his graphic instruction in the virtue of Benevolence. He is told to stand with his left foot across the lodge and his right foot down the lodge and yet turn his body to face and listen to the Master. Why this awkward stance?

The answer, of course, is because in a properly appointed lodge room the rough and smooth ashlars are placed at the North-East or South-East corner of the floor. When this happens the Initiate has to stand with his feet as instructed **round the sides** of the roughly-hewn stone placed there. It is thus appropriate for the Master to inform him that he is placed in this position to symbolise the beginning of the erection of any building. He starts with fashioning a stone to the required dimension.

What is puzzling, if you think about it, is the fact that he is also told that 'from the foundation laid this evening may you raise a super-structure perfect in all its parts.' Surely this must mean that what he also represents is a shaped and carefully prepared 'cornerstone' that was traditionally laid at the North-East point of the intended building? Yet he has a rough ashlar symbolically or actually between his feet. How can this be? I believe the answer is this. In ancient Freemasonry, the Apprentice was **first given** a rough ashlar to work on and when he could shape it into a smooth ashlar, he was then considered ready to be admitted a 'Fellow or Master of the Craft'. It was with the smooth ashlar in his hand that the Master addressed him and it was this that enabled him to be regarded as 'a just and upright Mason'. When the Speculative ceremonies were otherwise divided up the smooth ashlar became the sign of the Fellowcraft.

What are we to make of that strange object that sometimes occupies the top of the Senior Wardens pedestal or is placed on the floor in the West? It is usually a tripod with a pulley and chain suspending a smooth ashlar though in my own York lodge and elsewhere it is a more primitive hoist of another design.

The answer here is that it symbolically represents the 'raising of the Fellow or Master who made this stone' and where a tripod is used the further implication of **three being needed** to raise the object is clear. Moreover, the fact that it is on or near the Senior Warden's pedestal means that with the other ashlars in their proper positions we here have the apex of a triangle of progress through the several degrees. Again, I have to point out that all this helpful explanation is neglected by so many and thus the valuable symbolism of our furniture and its appointment is lost.

It was a similar object of great antiquity in Freemasonry that was almost lost entirely to view had it not been that about ten years ago the long memory of our English Grand Lodge was re-activated and the Trowel was returned to service. Much to the surprise of most Masons it was reintroduced as the collar jewel of the Charity Steward, an office that is now as much part of the officers' list as any other. But why the trowel and not a simulated cheque book or at least a box for collecting contributions?

Once more the answer is a neglected one. In the earliest days of English practice the trowel was often the jewel worn by the youngest new Apprentice when he took up his first duty as the ostensible Inner Guard of the Lodge. That latter title was not used until after the Union of our Grand Lodges and before that date he was known as the Inner Tyler. Being the newest member it was his task to make sure that when all duly qualified were assembled and that meant that he had to learn the password leading to the first degree (and how many know that?) he should then remember always to seal up the lodge (or make sure all the tiles to prevent eavesdroppers were in place, i.e. to tile it) and thence to be the first to welcome his immediate successor as the next candidate for the Craft. The Trowel he carried, either in his hand or on a ribbon, was the obvious symbol of privacy, security and fraternal brotherhood.

In the Royal Cumberland Lodge No. 41 of Bath we have the following and exceptional wording: the "trowel is used for the noble and glorious purpose of **spreading the cement of Brotherhood** and affection which unites us in a sacred bond as a Society of Brethren amongst whom no contention should ever exist." This, I know, is still wording that is used in some American lodges and is clearly not neglected there. It surely explains the use of the Trowel for 'Charity' and once explained seems natural to Masons. It also suggests the origin of one kind of 'fire' at table.

What should also be known is that still in some Irish lodges the trowel is the implement presented to the Candidate at the North-East corner when he is asked if he has anything to give in the cause of charity. When you realise that this was also the implement used in ancient working to be presented to the naked left breast of the candidate on entry the use of it as a trowel points to his heart, reminding him of the need for charity, is even more telling.

What is no less important is the fact that the trowel's use by the newest apprentice at last fully explains those otherwise peculiar words:

"Monarchs themselves have not thought it derogatory to their dignity to exchange the Sceptre for the Gavel." Oh: isn't that correct? But surely Kings would exchange their sign of rule in the world for the sign of rule in the Lodge? **But NO:** what the ritual is saying is much more searching. An earthly ruler is not ashamed to assume the role of the newest and most junior of all Masons and to hold the Trowel at the Lodge's door. How could we neglect such important teaching? Well, it may interest you to know that somewhere else in England, they don't. In the oldest Lodge in Norwich they still give the latest Apprentice a silver trowel to wear.

I have said enough to make my point, I believe, and I am sure that as you gather on this or any other lodge evening you will begin to ask yourselves what else have we neglected to make this Masonry of ours less fascinating than it ought to be. I would love to pursue the matter with you but it is time to call a halt. I can only wish for you further worthwhile hours as you discover the hidden because neglected recesses of nature and science.

The Puzzle of the Third Degree

Does the title of this address itself puzzle you? It certainly intrigued your Secretary when I suggested it to him for this evening. Yet though I am all for interesting titles this one is not meant simply to attract attention. It represents for me a serious and quite long-standing bewilderment – how, why and for what do we have this strange Masonic oddity the Master Mason's degree?

But wait a moment, I can hear some of you thinking, what is so odd about the third Degree? We have had it in English, Scottish and Irish Freemasonry for at least 270 years, we practise it in our own lodge faithfully once or twice a year and we see it performed in the other lodges we visit, most of us know it almost off by heart and it would be unthinkable to progress in the Craft without being raised to this sublime degree. Where is the puzzle? What are you, I hear you asking, you who have been a Master Mason for nearly 50 years, going on about?

That is also a very proper question and I am so pleased that you should allow me time to try to answer your own puzzlement.

Let me begin by laying out for you **FIVE** questions that have dogged me throughout my Masonic career and have only in recent years begun to receive an explanation that satisfies me. There are certainly several other queries that ought to be raised but five is enough for this evening and quite enough to show you why the Third Degree has always seemed to me such a puzzle.

The first thing is this. Why is this the only degree in Freemasonry that has what are called '*substituted* words, signs and tokens'? As one who has passed through the Chair of every other British degree, I know this to be a fact and it is one that has always amazed me. The puzzle is *why do we not receive* what we are told in the opening ceremony of the degree is to be our purpose? Let me remind you:

W.M. "From whence come you?

J.W. From the East.

W.M. Whither directing your steps? (Some say, your course)

S.W. To the West.

W.M. What inducement have you to leave the East and go to the West?

J.W. To seek for *that which is lost* which by *your instruction* and our own industry *we hope to find.*

W.M. What is that which is lost?

S.W. The *genuine secrets* of a Master Mason . . .

W.M. Where do you hope to *find them*?

S.W. With the Centre (some rituals say – *On* the Centre) . . and the W.M. concludes: "*I will assist* you to **repair that loss** . . ."

So when we start every Third Degree we are hopeful and even encouraged to look forward to what – in every other degree is the quite natural and satisfying result of the ceremony through which we have paid our initiation fee to pass . . . the *true secrets* of this degree. But what is the result of all our labours? Hear the closing:

W.M. Bro. J.W. whence come you?

J.W. From the West, W.M., whither we have *travelled* in search of *the genuine secrets* of a Master Mason.

W.M. Have you found them?

S.W. We *have not*, W.M. . . .

Why, I repeat, is this the only degree in the whole of Freemasonry where *you do not achieve* what you initially set out to do in the Opening?

Puzzle No. 2. What exactly is going on when we hear the Junior Warden in the opening say that he, or the Master Masons he represents, come *from the East*, when he is standing in the South, whilst the Senior Warden says that he represents those who leave the East and *go to the West*, when he is *already* in the West? Either they are both confused or they are suggesting something which is not being disclosed. And yet unless we know what they really mean, how can they, or we, hope to discover the expected genuine secrets of a Master Mason? I am indeed puzzled.

Puzzle No. 3. What is meant by the *following* further dialogue which we go through in the Opening ceremony?

W.M. Where do we hope to find **them**? (i.e. the genuine secrets?)

S.W. With the Centre.

W.M. What is a Centre? (some rituals say THE Centre)

J.W. A point within a circle from which all parts . . .

W.M. And why with the Centre?

S.W. Because that is a point from which a Master Mason *cannot* err.

Whatever is all this about? We are still talking seriously about the location of the spot where the genuine secrets of a Master Freemason are to be discovered. It is a matter of the most significant kind and yet our brethren talk in riddles. What Centre are we thinking about? Surely this is not just an occasion for a basic Geometry lesson – 'that point within a circle . . .'? There must be something more behind this which is not being revealed. So we have a double puzzle here – why do they use such cryptic words and just what is it that they are referring to?

And what about 'the point from which a Master Mason *cannot err?*' Whatever does that mean? Even when we might at last agree where and what the Centre point is, does this next phrase mean that Master Masons cannot wander off from it, or is it some moral point from which they will not deviate? I hope you can see why I, and I suspect may others, find this whole 3° opening a puzzle.

Puzzle No. 4. Nor is that all. When the question is asked 'How came the genuine secrets to be lost?' the answer is 'By the untimely death of our Grand Master, H.Ab . . .' Now here is a puzzle. If we do not know what the genuine secrets are, how can we ever hope to find them if they were lost by the death of the important person who had them? One might deduce that there could be three answer to the riddle.

One is that there were other people who knew them even if Hiram Abiff had died, but if so, who were they? A second is that anyone who passes *through the same experience* as he did may perhaps be allowed to learn those genuine secrets. A third possibility is that whilst they were lost with his death, they might *still be around somewhere* if we only look. After all a gold pocket watch on a murdered person is probably only lost until someone searches the dead man's clothing. But the complicated puzzle remains: which is the right way to solve this mystery of the loss or is there yet another way still not mentioned?

Puzzle No. 5. Just what does being a *Master Mason* mean? It doesn't give you real answers such as you have in the first two degrees. Being a F.C. was all that was necessary to become a Warden and hence a Master of a Lodge and to this day we start the Ceremony of Installation in the F.C. degree and take obligations for the Chair there. Yet when we move into the M.M. Degree it is only in order to throw the Master Masons out. So, a Master Mason is in fact no better off than a F.C. What then is the point of being a Master Mason? The puzzles of the degree continue.

So now I have spent 15 minutes showing you some of the real puzzles that attach to this degree. Of course some Masons do not find any of this puzzling because they simply do not ask themselves what they are saying and doing. They just go through the motions and that is why we find ourselves in such a difficulty when anyone outside the Craft asks us what it is really all about. We honestly don't know because when we do begin to think about it, *it is even* a puzzle for us.

For myself, spending a lifetime just playing with a puzzle simply will not do. I need answers . It may be that you will not agree with the answers – or some of them – that I am going to offer to the puzzles just noted, and if you have your own answers I shall be glad to hear them. What I think is important is that I hope I shall have got all of us to think afresh about what we do in the Master Mason degree rather than just repeating it parrot fashion. So here goes, and of course because time is limited, as in any lecture, I shall give you a *brief* explanation and if there any queries about it afterwards please feel free to question me further.

We know for a fact that when the Premier Grand Lodge adapted ancient Freemasonry to its new Speculative shape it only allowed an Apprentice ceremony and a Master or Fellow of the Craft degree for the normal Mason. Indeed at first, the Premier Grand Lodge *alone* could confer the Fellow or Master of the Craft degree (for it had both names) and Lodges could only obligate apprentices. By **1723** however the number of lodges had grown and so Grand Lodge allowed private lodges to confer the F.C. degree themselves. It was, let me assure you, a much more interesting and instructive degree than the one which we have today.

But the Grand Lodge still kept something else to itself, as the old Operatives had always done. This was the Installation of a Master Mason in the Chair, at least at the start of a **new** lodge. Thereafter, the Master would know, with other Past Masters, how to conduct the ceremony of 'raising a Master' in the future. That was what being **a real Master** was all about. But what happened?

From the year 1726 there had begun to be a demand, especially by brethren of noble birth or civic importance, for something more than the degree of F.C. They wanted a degree superior to that of mere **trade mastery**. From at least **1730** a re-designed but *incomplete* 'Master's Part', though with *substituted* secrets, was being offered to candidates both in existing lodges as well as in what were now called 'Master's Lodges'.

This new 'Third Degree' was available even for those who were not necessarily to become rulers in the Craft or reigning Masters of lodges. Acquiring this new degree did not, as I have already said, enable a Fellowcraft to have more access to the Chair nor, until the early 19th century, admit its holders to the Royal Arch. The development meant that certain secrets and practices belonging to *real Masters* were liable to be veiled, laid aside or neglected, and Canon Tydeman in the 1971 Prestonian Lecture most strikingly drew attention, as I have already done, to the anomalies in the present working that were the result. The truth was that because this new degree was carved out of a working in which the now undisclosed and *genuine secrets* of the Master's Part were conferred these latter had now to be conveyed in some *other Masonic fashion* and place. It is the contention of this paper that it was this necessity that (i) led to the puzzles in what we now have, and (ii) gave rise to the emergence of a separate ceremony of Installation, to the Scots Master degree, the Harodim, Royal Order, Arch and Royal Arch ceremonies.

It is here that we might seem to encounter a difficulty. If the way to solve the puzzles belongs to those who belong to other degrees, how can we expect to discover it without requiring those in those degrees to violate an obligation. For example, if part of the solution to our 3° puzzle can be revealed by what happens at the Installation of the Master of a Lodge how can those below that rank expect to be enlightened? No one who has become such a Lodge Master can reveal the secrets of that ceremony to those not so entitled to it. The same may be said of those who are Royal Order or Royal Arch members. Are we then placed in an impossible and intractable situation? The answer today has to be 'no, we are not'. Let me explain.

The first intimation of what we now call our Master Mason's degree, at a time when ritual books were not so much frowned on as not even thought of, was by a public exposure called

"Masonry Dissected" by a man called Prichard, who claimed to have been through the ceremony as a Mason. So for over 260 years the public have had access to what we get up to in the 3°. Yet in a letter of **1738** which was written by a Mason using the name 'Euclid' and which was attached to the official Constitutions of that year, we read as follows:

"Many valuable things could not come to (Prichard) the Dissector's knowledge for that they are not intrusted with any Brothers **till after due Probation**", which means that there were known to be other, genuine?, secrets yet in store for appropriate Masons. And on this letter, an Irish Masonic scholar, Dr Philip Crossle, writes:

"Prichard may be likened to one who 'after due Probation' was **not found worthy** to proceed to the real degree of 'Master, or Master of the Company' nor to discover the profound and sublime things of **old Masonry**." (Irish Research Lodge, p.186.)

What is clear therefore is that there was at that time more to know. Can we discover what it may have been? Yes, we can, because we now have the details of two rituals both of which are, as such, no longer parts of regular degrees conferred today and thus involve no obligation and which have been known to Masonic scholars for at least a century. The trouble is that they have not been known by most Masons. What do they reveal to us?

From **1730**, we know that in the 'Master Lodges' in which the new 3° was to be conferred, there appeared a superior group called *Scots Masters* who wore hats, as did Installed Masters and who always sat in the East like the other lodge rulers, wore collarettes or sashes with a special medallion and claimed to have superior knowledge, viz. the 'genuine secrets' of this Master's degree. In a French exposure of this 'Ecossais' degree we have the following short catechism:

Q: Are you an Ecossais Master?
A: I was brought out of the captivity of Babylon.
Q: Who honoured you with the degree of Ecossais?
A: Prince Zerubbabel, of the line of David and Solomon.
Q: When?
A: Seventy years after the destruction of the holy city.
Q: In what are the Ecossais Masons occupied?
A: In rebuilding the Temple of God.
Q: Why do the Ecossais Masons carry the sword and buckler? (or shield).
A: In memory of the order given to all workmen at the time of the rebuilding of the Temple, to have swords always at their sides and their bucklers near at hand, for use in case of attack by their enemies."

So now we have Masons who are superior to 3° Masons and who have come from the East to the West – Babylon to Jerusalem – to complete the work of building the Temple again and doing so *with the assistance* of the Prince and ruler who is in the line of Solomon. Some of the puzzles of the 3° opening begin to be clarified.

Let us turn to the other 'Master's degree' practised at the Ben Jonson tavern in Spitalfields, London? Why was it that when some Moderns Master Masons came to visit this listed Moderns lodge in 1755 they were not allowed entry? Could it have been because, as we shall shortly see, the members here were practising what no mere 3° Mason was entitled to share? Well, the refusal of those visitors led to the Lodge being erased by the Premier Grand Lodge, so it must have been something special.

The degree in question had been conferred in this lodge since the **1730**s at least. It was made up of two distinct parts that were seen as one whole. The R.W. Master, representing Solomon, was robed in scarlet, was crowned and carried a sceptre; the S.W. wore a purple robe, was also crowned, had a sceptre and represented Hiram of Tyre; whilst the J.W. had a sable garment, held a rod and took the part of Hiram A.B. They are thus shown in the frontispiece of 'Ahiman Rezon', (the Antients G.Lo. Constitutions) and are there accompanied by Moses, Aholiab and Bezaleel, with Zerubbabel, Haggai and Joshua, all clad in a similar manner. In the Ben Jonson Lodge working, however, these latter persons did not figure. The Lodge was opened *in the F.C. degree* and when that ceremony was completed, the S.W. withdrew, leaving his chair vacant.

The candidates were admitted and after some preliminary ceremonies which included a word beginning with 'J' as a test word for others present, the Guide asked the J.W. to honour the promise made some time ago. "Our works are now completed and we accordingly seek admission amongst *Geometrick Masters* of the Craft." To this the J.W. replied that sadly the duties of Dedicating the Temple had prevented the King from doing for them what was promised. Having been encouraged to seek the Sovereign Grand Master themselves they ask that as the Temple has been finished and dedicated to the 'true and everliving God, whose name be exalted,' they should have "the distinguished reward of being admitted to the honourable and sublime degree of Geometrick Master Masons". This is acknowledged by Solomon as a proper request but he explains that as King Hiram of Tyre has had to depart, and the degree can only be conferred when the three 'rulers' are present, the Craftsmen are told:

"If you are willing to take upon yourselves the obligation of a *Master Mason* and await the return of our royal ally, we may thus far comply with your request." The Guide answered, "Sire, we very joyfully accept your most gracious offer, and confess ourselves extremely grateful." The password 'J' is given with the explanation that it means 'Eternal habitation' (originally 'Zabulon'), the obligation is administered together with certain signs, including one given "at the transgression of our first parents and by Moses in the wilderness of Sinai", and the Lodge is then called from labour to refreshment.

The second part of the degree recounted the loss **and recovery** of the Sacred Word and began with the S. W. now appearing in the west. The candidates again approach the R.W. Master, informing him that as King Hiram is returned, they claim "the high and sublime mysteries of a Geometrick Master Mason". The R.W. Master now notices that the *J.W's place is vacant* and on enquiring where he may be is told that he is probably still at his devotions as was his custom at High Meridian. A search about the Temple is made in the course of which they **reveal the Arch** with the Ark of the Covenant beneath it and there **recover the Lost Word.**

The R.W.M. then addresses the candidates thus:

"We permitted our lamented Brother, after casting the two Pillars of the Porch, to engrave the mysterious Word upon a plate of gold within the figure of our signet, and to wear it as a mark of our royal favour and good will, and I have no doubt but it is still in his possession."

There then follows the discovery of the body of Hiram (which is represented by the J.W. lying on the floor with a sprig of evergreen at his head) and as the body is raised by the Master, S.W. *and others present*, the medallion is taken from within the J.W's inner pocket. (Its design is not unlike an emblem that appears on a R.A. certificate today.) The medallion was set on the Holy Bible in place of the square and compasses on the altar *at the centre of the lodge*, which was then its normal position, and the Brethren having been seated, the R.W. Master delivered a charge, a lecture and an address. (The whole of these are recorded in Dr Oliver's 'Origin of the Holy Royal Arch' pp.93-104). I will only draw attention briefly to four interesting extracts which link up with so much that we have noticed already in this paper:

i.   "Brethren, we are peculiarly fortunate in the recovery of this jewel, containing the mysterious Word, which would otherwise have been irrecoverably lost . . . What indeed could be more appropriate as a gift to those who assisted in erecting a House to His Glory than the true name of the Great Creator . . ."

ii.   And that you may for ever bear in mind the sad scene you have just witnessed, let me exhort you to humble yourselves to the final condition of mortality that you may be raised on the SIX points of fellowship . . ." (These were explained as relating to the Seal of Solomon, and the sixth point was 'mouth to ear to warn each other'.)

iii.   "I will therefore present you with the working tools of a Master Mason which are, every one of them, implements of Masonry, and especially **the trowel**. After the stones intended for a building have been hewn and properly squared **the trowel** is used by operative Masons for uniting them together by means of cement."

iv.   "You are also, my Brethren, entitled, as Master Masons, to the use of an alphabet . . . it is geometrick in its character, and is therefore eminently useful to Master Masons in general." (The cypher system is then explained.)

It is when you are introduced to this kind of 'Masters degree' that you begin to realise why your own 3° seems so incomplete. It was bound to be incomplete because it was missing some vital components which were restricted to true Masters of Lodges. You can also appreciate why ordinary Master Masons were refused entry. Now, at least, you can better appreciate what it was that the opening of the present Master Mason's degree was meant to lead to and what seemed puzzles are just inducements to search a little further. If you want to know how more fully to complete the degrees you have, then I am sure there are those in this lodge who can help you.

But of course you may be content to just go on being puzzled.

Unknown Parts of the Tracing Boards

T he title of this paper may perhaps surprise some of those who have gathered to receive it. Surely, it might be said, the tracing boards are there for us all to see, there are lectures available (even if they are not always or regularly given) which explain the boards, and most of us have already lived with them sufficiently for them to be familiar if not well-known. How then can any parts of them be 'unknown'? Well, it is my belief that there are such unknown parts and enquiry of many Masons on every continent has confirmed me in saying that lack of knowledge about them exists. It even reveals itself when we seek to determine which tracing boards that are presently used we are going to examine.

Would you believe, for example, that *not every board* from the earliest Harris board of the 1820s to the present has *the same* following features:

$1°$: The symbols on or above the ladder rising from the pedestal;
The arrangement of the three pillars;
The kind of trestle board or drawing plan;
The design on the front of the pedestal.
$2°$: The number of people shown in the picture;
The nature of the chambers above or below the stairs;
The number of steps on the staircase;
The place where the great pillars stand.
$3°$ The placing of a sprig of acacia;
The intimation, or otherwise, of a grave;
The figures on the coffin top.
The design of the dormer over the doorway, if there is one.

This mere recital of variations, and these are not the only ones as you will shortly see, must convince any student of tracing boards in the post **1820** period that there are ample unknown parts to be acquainted with. So that we may focus on the same design I have chosen the Emulation trio.

The First Degree Tracing Board

TRACING BOARD—FIRST DEGREE

At first glance this picture may appear to present few surprises but before I come to the three items that I would suggest are 'unknown', I must point out some peculiarities of this design. The pedestal is marked with a circle having a point at its centre but the parallel lines that are customary when this figure is displayed are not shown. Moreover, the point within a circle is surely a symbol referred to in the 3° and yet it appears here in the 1°. Similarly we note the square, level and plumbrule which are properly associated with the 2°. There is no rough ashlar, unless the stone 'mound', with a small maul or gavel upon it, is meant to represent that item, but we do have a squared ashlar and one with a cramp or 'lewis' in it. This too has definite 3° links though the presence of the chisel could be said to refer to the 1° working tools. Lastly, the trestle board in front of the pedestal has no drawing on it.

Turning to the features that I suggest are wholly or comparatively unknown, we have (a) the mosaic pavement; (b) a fourth symbol on the ladder; and (c) the four tassels at the corners. Let me deal with these in turn.

The Mosaic Pavement

Masons generally are familiar with the explanation of this feature as representing the diverse character of the life we lead with its dark and light periods, its difficulties and achievements, its promises and disappointments. But that is explaining its symbolism. What its origin was and why it has been deemed so important and essential from the earliest use, not only of tracing boards but of lodge carpet decoration, is not explained. It is that which might well be termed 'unknown'.

Freemasonry in Britain has always been associated in some way with the Temple of King Solomon. The lodge room itself represent some part of that structure, the Master himself stands for that monarch, incidents in the course of completing the building of the Temple are referred to in the several degrees and in the consecration of every new Masonic lodge, direct connection with the Temple hallowing is always invoked. It is therefore not surprising that in each of the three tracing boards, and not only in the 1°, there should be something that directly relates to that edifice. That 'something' is the squared black and white flooring. The reason why there is such a connection is as follows.

In the middle of the 16th century, after Henry VIII had at last reluctantly accepted the need for a Bible in the 'vulgar tongue', that is, in English, new translations of the scriptures began to flourish. In 1560, after the short reign of Queen Mary, there was published a Bible that was called the **Geneva version**, because the translators of it had been exiles in that city when it was being produced. One of the new features of this particular Bible were its illustrations, the first such to appear in any Bible in England. These illustrations were all, of course, in black and white since no printing press for some centuries could produce the coloured pictures of the earlier monastic manuscripts.

What is important for our purposes is to note that whenever the Temple of Solomon, or even Solomon's house and throne, are shown in these pages the floor is always depicted as made up of black and white chequered squares. Thus was born the 17th century idea that this was the correct indication of the Temple of Solomon. You might give it medieval towers, characters in medieval dress, and even a long Christian type altar but you made sure that your readers knew it was the Temple of Solomon by the black and white flooring. When the designers of the first floorcloths or floor drawings, and then tracing boards, for Masons had to depict the Temple or a reference to it, there was no alternative. The mosaic pavement was the only option. It was called 'Mosaic' because in that same Bible the precursor of the Temple was the Tabernacle in the wilderness built by Moses' command on God's instructions. The floor of that same holy meeting place was also always shown as black and white squares. The Temple mosaic pavement was born. It is with us still.

The Key On The Ladder

The number of symbols shown on the ladder here is itself a generally unknown feature. Whilst some versions have the figures of angels who are ascending or descending, as in the original story from the Bible, of Jacob's Ladder, it is much more usual for there to be only three items, though these can vary considerably in position and form.

In this design, we have a fourth symbol – the key – placed between the cross of faith and the anchor of hope. These two latter virtues, joined by the chalice of 'charity' at the apex, reflect what was, on the oldest tracing boards, a three-runged ladder. It is indeed these three virtues that are explained in the lecture that was written to accompany this same board. What, however, is the point of the Key, which is not explained?

The answer to this question begins with something very old in terms of Craft ritual. In the Edinburgh Register House MS. of 1696, as well as other texts of that period, we have the following:

Q: Which is the key of your lodge?
A: A weel hung tongue.

Many of the early texts expanded this key/tongue connection and added that the key was lodged in a 'bone box' (which meant the mouth) and that a true Mason kept this box securely locked. It was precisely this idea that was illustrated in the 'Masonic' opera by Mozart, 'Die Zauberflöte' when the garrulous Papageno is subjected to the indignity of having a padlock clamped on his lips to keep him silent.

In the Sloane MS. of around 1700, we have the key explained in terms of a phrase that has now become part of the 1° password:

Q: What is the Keys of your Lodge Doore made of?
A: It is not made of Wood Stone Iron or steel or any sort of mettle but the **tongue of a good report** behind a brother's back as well as before his face.

If with this first mention of 'free and of good report' we can recognise the key as related to the 1° we are also reminded that in the Charge to the Initiate we use the words:

"Still, however, as a Freemason, there are other excellences of character to which your attention may be peculiarly and forcibly directed: among the foremost of these are **secrecy** . . ." and you know the rest. Moreover, as the three other virtues on the rungs are of scriptural provenance, so we ought also to remember the biblical injunction: 'Let not your right hand know what your left hand doeth' – discretion in one's charitable dealings is also the key to a true Freemasonry.

The Four Tassels
These apparently discreet attachments to the board are often thought to be explained by attaching them to the four virtues also mentioned in the 1° Charge – prudence, temperance, fortitude

and justice. That, as with the pavement, is fine for explaining the symbolism but does not explain its origin and additional importance.

In first considering the erection of any edifice, the architect had to select a site and then mark out the line for the foundations. This he did by fixing pegs at the four corners and attaching a cord or string from one peg to another. Thus the area was enclosed and the line of the walls determined. Where the cord or string was tied round each peg there was created a knot that was later formalised and became the tassel at each corner. In forming their 'lodge', the architect-Masons quite literally established its dimensions by the lines and tassels that they could see. In exactly the same way the dimensions of the lodge are still defined by the lines of the board and the tassels at its corners. This is why, when a new lodge is due to be consecrated, the order is given at one part of the ceremony, "Let the board be uncovered", and the tracing board, with its tassels, is laid bare in the centre of the floor and is then duly 'dedicated' by the pouring of corn, wine and oil upon it – for it is thus representing the new lodge itself. It is still at that point without human members who have yet to be themselves purged with salt before being constituted as the latest 'Lodge No . . .'

So significant are the tassels considered to be as defining the limits of the lodge that in older English and Welsh halls the tassels are hung from the four corners of the ceiling, thus ensuring that everyone present is 'within the lodge'. Otherwise, with the tassels only on the mosaic 'carpet', it might be said that the members were sitting around, but outside, the lodge.

In the USA and parts of Canada, the lodge is actually defined as the modest area of mosaic 'carpet' with tassels that lies in the middle of the room westward of the central pedestal or altar. No-one may cross or step onto that area which is the fixed replica of the consecrated 'lodge'. To emphasise this point, I have seen on that continent tassels actually drawn out in relief from each corner of the carpet so as to emphasise its presence. In view of what was said earlier about the origin of the *mosaic* carpet it is also interesting to remember that it was tassels which were worn by the priests in the service of God in the Temple of Solomon. Such then are some unknown parts of the 1° Tracing Board.

The Second Degree Tracing Board

Like its predecessor, this board may at first glance appear straightforward and without any peculiarities. Yet a more careful examination reveals that its arrangement shows three distinct chambers, a lower, a middle and an upper and the latter is fenced in with a lattice which speaks clearly to any Mark Mason about the payment of wages. That, after all, is what these side storerooms in the original Temple of Solomon were partly created for and throughout the 18th century we have rituals which refer to the fact that apprentices went to receive their wages in a lower, the Fellowcrafts in a middle and the Master Masons in an upper chamber.

We might also notice that above the curtained entrance to the middle chamber, and under the inner arch, appear certain Hebrew characters that are not normally revealed until we have completed the 3° in the Royal Arch, whilst beneath that sacred tetragrammaton, representing the Deity, there is a dove in a singularly evocative form. It is not like that usually seen at the

71

Ark of Noah or on the deacons' wands, but in medieval pictures of the Trinity. Above the outer arch of this central area there are also the cherubim usually associated with the Sanctum Sanctorum of the 3°. Let us, however, turn to three even more 'unknown' parts of this board.

The Steps Of The Staircase

Has it ever occurred to you to ask why there should be '15 or more steps' on the staircase in the 2°? Pragmatists might say that it is because we refer to the symbolism of 3, 5 and 7 steps in the ritual and these add up to the required number. The answer, I believe, is much more interesting than that. It has, once more, a reference back to the Temple at Jerusalem.

Medieval legend included a story called 'The Presentation in the Temple' that was actually performed as one of the cycle of mystery plays in the City of Coventry. This performance showed Mary, the child of Joachim and Anna and the later mother of Jesus, being brought as a young girl to be blessed and having to mount a ceremonial stairway made up of 15 steps which led to the High Priest who sat on a throne at the top of them in the inner Temple. There are manuscript and stained glass representations of this interesting event and, in some of these pictures the stairs are even divided up into stages of 3, 5 and 7. What is more we are given the very words the actor representing Mary had to say when the stairs were being climbed. I cannot reproduce all the verses in this paper but the following are strangely significant for their influence on later Masonic practice. It should be recalled that in Latin, 'gradus' means both 'step' and 'degree'. The girl stops 3 times as she mounts:

"The fyrst degre, gostly applied, It is holy desyre with God to be, In trobyl to God I have cryed . . ." (The first degree charge?)

"The secunde is stody, with meke inquyssyon veryly.

How I shall have knowynge of Gods wylle . . ." (The South-East charge?)

"The thrydde is gladness in minde in hope to be That we shall be savyd all thus . . ." (The 3° experience?)

What struck me even more when I first read this Coventry play was that when the maiden reached the top of the stairs the High Priest reminds her of the Ten Commandments and then tells her that each day she is 'to serve God with prayer, devote some of her time to manual labour, and take 'a resonable tyme to fede'. An interesting direction before she is admitted to the Temple.

The Location Of The Staircase

As I became more and more familiar with the arrangement of the Temple of Solomon and then tried to relate that to our ritual it increasingly puzzled me why there seemed to be some discrepancy between them. Why, for instance, is there an opening on the South side of the Temple (with the two great pillars that ought to be at the East entrance) when there is no mention in the Bible or commentaries of any such opening in an outer wall? Moreover, if the opening is to the South on our board, they why does the staircase run South to West when we take a candidate North to East? Even if the pillars show that the opening is actually the Temple's porchway or entrance then why does the staircase run East to South when we do something else? It seems odd and unnecessarily confusing. Is there something we do not know? The answer is, Yes, there is.

What the Bible tells us is that there was an opening in the South wall *of the Holy Place* and that of course led to the chambers on three floors at the side of the Temple. Some versions of the 2° tracing board actually show this and then we see something very different. The staircase then leads from the **North** side of the bottom floor of the side chambers up in a true spiral stairway

towards the East end of the middle floor. We are actually going in the very same direction as we perform in our ritual. If, in the picture before us, the staircase began at the wall where the lowest arches are and then spiralled round as it does the same effect would be achieved. But that is only understood when you know how the original access to the various side-chambers was explained in the Bible. What we tend to do is rely too much on what our later designers thought was right rather than going to the proper sources.

An Ear Of Corn Near To A Fall Of Water

It would be a strange tracing board for this degree which did not today carry a scene incorporating these two features. Yet for a long period in my Masonry, there were two questions that dogged me: how could one word signify two such different things and why was such a word used to protect the crossing of the river Jordan? I now know the answer.

The earliest Semitic word we know for 'an ear of corn' was spelt s.b.l.t. which explains why Arabic, Ephraimite and earlier Hebrew, the word was pronounced either 'sibolet' or 'seblit'. The early Semitic word for a watercourse or the 'way' the water ran was 'sh.b.l' which became the early Hebrew word 'shebil'. Somehow, and scholars still do not know why or when, the speakers of non-Ephraimite Hebrew began to use the same word for 'an ear of corn' and a 'channel of water' and called it **shiblot**. In case you find this surprising, may I remind you that we do the same in English. The word 'shift' can mean 'a garment', a 'movement of earth', a 'period of work', and even a 'typewriter movement'. It is only the context that helps to clarify the meaning. The answer to my first query is now possible. Sh . . . th does not **mean** 'an ear of corn near to a fall of water', but is 'depicted' as such because the Hebrew word could mean either of these items separately.

What is also fascinating is that in Modern Arabic, the original old word 'sh.b.l' meaning 'a way' has now become 'sabil' so that in Islamic practice, the word 'sabil' means '**a way** of charity.' The word also means 'a fountain' and this fits perfectly with its other meaning for there is no greater act of charity in the desert than to provide *water* for a traveller on his *way*.

We can now begin to see the suitability of the word used in this degree. The Hebrew guards of the water crossing ask the approaching Ephraimite travellers for the word that means 'I would pass by the water way' (sabil) but the guards call it 'shebil' which small 'variation discovered their country' of origin. What you should also know is that on **pre-1813** tracing boards there is displayed, beside the ear of corn, a bridge over a flowing river (the Jordan) that could thus be guarded. There even developed a Red Cross degree called the 'Jordan Pass'.

The Third Degree Tracing Board

The only thing that is distinctive about this board is that the entrance to the Sanctum Sanctorum is formed by a series of columns rather than a simple doorway. The writing in Hebrew above

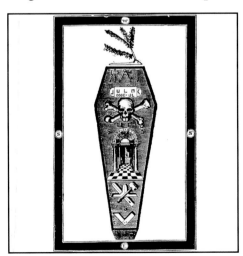

it is not always present and the words there translated as 'Holiness to the Lord' are usually associated with the Ark of the Covenant rather than with the doorway to it. Perhaps the artist felt that this was its most convenient place. Let us however turn one more time to the more 'unknown' features.

The Cypher Writing

If there is a mystery about anything in modern day Freemasonry it is the presence of, and yet the silence about, this cypher writing. As I have recently written about it at length elsewhere I must avoid making this paper too lengthy but it is a constant surprise to me that Master Masons readily accept this facet of the 3° Board without ever being given any information upon it. That it was most commonly associated with the Mark Master degree for over a century and is now only really preserved on that degree's tracing board and this one is itself a mystery. Let us at least make three brief comments upon it so it is not wholly unknown.

First: it took its rise from the employment of a simple arrangement of crossed parallel lines in which the angles or sides of the spaces thus created represented letters of the alphabet. It was thus used in private, especially diplomatic, correspondence from at least the late 15th century and one user of it was no less a person than Cardinal Wolsey.

Secondly: Dots, diagonal lines, and even the diamond and the swastika, were further employed to diversify and extend the cypher use. It had been used in Service Intelligence and it may have been in such a setting that Dunckerley, as a naval officer, first encountered it. He introduced it to the Chapter of Friendship in Portsmouth.

Thirdly: Dr Oliver was to reveal several forms of the alphabet in his book, 'The Origin of the Royal Arch', but it was Bro. Haunch in his AQC 75 article on Tracing Boards who explained the Harris board's cyphers. They read: T (H A B A L 3000) C, and below M B. Now at least we know.

The Three '5's

These figures are also displayed but few if any know why they are there or to what they allude. They are in fact mentioned, if only in passing, by the person narrating the traditional history of this degree, and then it is in two connections. We hear first of the 15 trusty Fellowcrafts who were appointed to make diligent search for the Master Architect – and it is here that I would remind you why the tools of the 3° are those of an Architect and not a working Mason – and hence the division into 3 parties of 5 going (and here notice the different orientation of this board) North, East and South. Later we are told that the Master was buried in a grave 5 feet from North and South and 5 feet or more perpendicular (persons then being buried upright to await the general resurrection). Thus we have the explanation of otherwise puzzling items. What should also be said is that on some boards the 5th letter of the Hebrew alphabet replaces these Western numerals. The connections with 5 are thus retained but now we have a further triangle made up of the letters that refer to the eternal attributes of the Almighty.

The Parted Curtain Of The Sanctuary

If the cypher characters constitute the major mystery of this board then the parted curtain certainly hints at another. We know to what sacred portion of the Temple these curtains gave admittance and the words above the colonnaded doorway tell us of the Ark but apart from recognising the right of the High Priest to enter there 'and that only once a year' it is difficult to see why **in this degree** there should be any indication of truths yet to be revealed when even the Master Architect himself could not be buried in the Holy Place and certainly not in this place of divine darkness and silence. If the veil is to be lifted then it is in another place and at another time in Masonry that such is to happen. Could it be that here the Master Mason is being beckoned to yet one more step that he ought to take and that he will then enter the most Holy place of all where God in glory reigns? Could it even be that here there is the remnant of that earlier Christian Masonry in which, after the slaying and raising of another Master the veil of the Temple was torn aside and the Sanctum Sanctorum laid open to view? That is something we have still to know. It leaves us at least realising that despite all our familiarity with these tracing boards there are still unknown parts of them for us to pursue.

Was there ever such a change?

It is sometimes remarked in the latter years of the 20th century that there has been far too much change in the practice of the Craft. For those who only have their sights on the differences in Masonry between 1950 and 1999, the complaint – and it usually is a complaint – might seem to have some justification. Yet the truth is that from the time when the Premier Grand Lodge in 1717 began to alter and adapt what had been the practice of such Freemasonry as existed previously change has been at work in some parts, and during most periods of the Craft's existence. As used to be said in an organisation for which I once used to work, "Constant change has come to stay".

Yet there was one period in the Craft's existence when perhaps the most profound changes occurred that English Freemasonry has ever known and they came about in a very short period of time. I refer of course to the years that followed upon the historic union of the hitherto separated Grand Lodges known as those of the Moderns and the Antients, which had existed from 1717 and 1751 respectively. It was as a result of the agreement reached between those who negotiated their merger into one United Grand Lodge – a merger that has lasted until the present time – that real changes took place. It is of the alterations in the very appearance and style of Freemasonry that then occurred that the title of this lecture, "Was there ever such a Change?" might be considered a fair description. What the various facets of that change were forms the substance of what follows.

The principal change that then took place may have seemed to be one simply of a legal nature, but its implications were much more far-reaching than simply the words included in the Act of the Union. I refer to the declaration that henceforth the 'pure Ancient Masonry (of England) consists of three degrees, and no more; viz. those of the Entered Apprentice, the Fellow Craft and the Master Mason (including the Supreme Order of the Holy Royal Arch)'. At first sight this may now seem to most Masons the most natural and obvious statement of the way things ought to be. That is because the steps taken by the Duke of Sussex and those responsible with him for the well-governing of the Craft were generally so effective that, today, the great majority of Freemasons would not only consider this statement to be true but would even wonder why those who formed the Union even bothered to include the Order of the Holy Royal Arch.

Yet that was not the effect which soon became apparent when this article of the Union began to be implemented. At least half of the then existing lodges in England were accustomed to a very different way of looking at their Freemasonry. On the one hand they believed that whilst it was customary for every Mason to progress through the three basic degrees they also believed that to receive the degree of the Holy Royal Arch was essential in order to complete one's Masonic career.

The way to that degree was by several other essential steps of which the degree of being installed in a Craft chair or a parallel ceremony of 'Passing the Chair' were the principal ones. Some would have also expected candidates for the Royal Arch to be Mark and Mark Master Masons as well as being Excellent and Super Excellent brethren. The fact that there had been for at least half a century some recognition that Royal Arch Masons also recognised a link with Knight Templary and even Rose Croix has also to be acknowledged. When therefore all this Masonry, practised in every part of the British Isles, but also in every quarter of England, was now stated to be peripheral and without any status in antiquity, it was a severe change that had to be faced.

Moreover it had been customary for at least half the Masons in England to regard their Craft Lodge warrants as being all the authority which they needed in order to carry out the extended

Masonry to which I have just referred. Evidence of this fact is actually still around by reason of the kind of Opening ceremony that is used in degrees 'beyond the Craft'. The similarity is because the pre-Union assumption was that these other degrees were part of, and therefore must conform to, basic Craft lodge custom. To be suddenly made aware not only that such 'extra' degrees were not really essential, that they were not permitted to be practised under the Lodge warrant and that if they were to be carried on they would require additional means of authorisation was a change of fairly extreme proportions.

Within five years of the Union a letter was sent to the Duke of Sussex, Grand Master, from certain brethren of Lancashire, with the Deputy Provincial Grand Master as the principal signatory. The letter contained the following passage:

". . . we beg to observe, that we are under the fullest conviction that the Royal Arch is a component part of Craft Masonry, and consequently requires no other Authority, than a Craft warrant to render their Meeting perfectly legal, and agreeable to ancient Custom."

To show both how law abiding they sought to be but how strongly they felt to be their cause, they added the following:

"We therefore pray, that your Royal Highness will be pleased to make this Communication known to the members of the **United Grand Lodge** assembled at the next Quarterly Meeting, in order that our Opinions, if correct may be confirmed, or if erroneous, that they may be refuted."

It is no part of this lecture to enter further into what became known as the secession of the 'Grand Lodge of Wigan' but these opinions, so cogently expressed to the proper government of the Craft, surely help to register an attitude to a major change that has certainly not been reproduced since. This is because the changes that have subsequently transpired have just not been of anything like the same consequence.

Yet this regulation regarding the 'nature' of Freemasonry was by no means the only change that Freemasons then had to encompass. There were practical matters of administration and conduct that must have caused strong ripples of astonishment, if not downright dissatisfaction.

One of these was the changing of Lodge numbers. Anyone who wants to know what numbering meant to our Masonic ancestors ought to read the story of what happened when the Grand Lodge of Scotland was set up in 1735. Such was the intensity of feeling about being given due acknowledgement of their antiquity that not only did the Lodge of Edinburgh become No. 1 but Melrose demanded that it be No. 1**bis** and Aberdeen No. 1**ter** whilst the 'Old Mother' Kilwinning claimed the number 0; or was it O for original? Almost a century later, feelings could still run high when it was agreed in England 'that The two first Lodges under each Grand Lodge (shall) draw a lot in the first place for priority, and to which of the two Lot no. 1 shall fall, the other to rank as No. 2; and all the other Lodges shall fall in alternately." In the result the highest position was allotted to the 'Grand Masters Lodge', the senior lodge of the Antients from 1751, whereas the Lodge of Antiquity, one of the founding lodges of the Premier Grand Lodge in 1717, had to content itself with being in second place. That was change indeed and this would not be the only lodge that must have felt that unity amongst Freemasons was bought at some cost.

As there was this alteration in the numbering of lodges so there was also a new arrangement in regard to the selection of Chapters. Unable to believe that Royal Arch Masonry could no longer be conducted under a Craft warrant it now appeared that there was to be regulation as to how many Chapters would be allowed in any one area. Since the requirement of being a Past Master in the Craft for joining the Holy Royal Arch was likely to restrict the numbers of Masons available, it was now felt by the new Supreme Grand

Chapter to be more sensible if the number of Chapters was limited – to something like one Chapter per three or four local lodges. In itself the idea was obviously sensible, but in terms of contrast with past practice this was another change too far. For those who fervently believed, as did the members of former Antients lodges, that entry to the Royal Arch was the 'sumum bonum' of all preceding Masonry it was contrary to all their convictions to concede that any authority could so restrict any lodge in offering that opportunity to its members. This was another thorn in the side of such as those protesting Lancashire Masons.

And even that was not all. Within the next 20 years this same new Supreme Grand Chapter was going to change the ground of admission to the Holy Royal Arch and allow those who were but Master Masons to apply for membership. At a stroke this meant that the intervening steps including Installation or Passing the Chair and the three stages known as the Veils, were all rendered meaningless and unnecessary. Of course it meant that a whole new pool of potential Chapter membership was created but in the process some half of English practice was effectively scrubbed out. This too was a change the dimension of which involving as it did notable changes in Chapter ritual details, was immeasurably greater than anything we have witnessed since.

Another change, however, was no less striking. It was now required that the old practice of meeting in the lodge room around tables with the juxtaposition of dining and doing ritual was to cease. There was to be a clear line drawn between the two activities. More dignity, it was thought, might be accorded to ceremonies that ought not to be sullied with the dangers of overindulgence in food and drink, not to mention spittoons and chamber pots. Examples of the latter from the 18th century are certainly on view in not a few lodge museums.

Accordingly the tables no longer appeared when the lodge met for business with a ceremony to be conducted though bits of them had to be retained to provide what we call the pedestals of the Master and Wardens and for the desks of the Secretary and Treasurer. After the Lodge was closed the brethren either brought the tables in to dine in the same room or they repaired to some other room or place for their refreshment. The change in any case was substantial and doubtless led to many regrets about 'the old days'. What we need to understand is that despite the change Masons have always considered the two parts of the evening as belonging to each other and it remains the case that as the Master rules over the lodge business so he is also meant to rule at the dining board. He has always presided at both.

The change in this arrangement also meant that there was now the whole floor for the use of such items or drawings as the Lodge was accustomed to employ for the instruction and enlightenment of its members. Accordingly the drawings on the floor that had had to be fitted into an angle of the tables could now be provided on a fuller and more ample scale or more objects could then be laid out on the central floor of the lodge room. The idea of having more permanent tracing cloths and then boards began to catch on and as soon as a room became no longer rented but owned by the lodge a carpet could be provided. The furniture of the present sort of meeting place was almost in place.

Yet even this was not the end of the story. Just as the United Grand Lodge, and especially its Royal Grand Master, had secured the tidying up of the conduct of lodge business so there were also proposed new forms of dress. What these were I have looked at in some detail in another lecture about Clothing but it is necessary that we record here two points that link in with what we have already considered.

The first point is that in order to drive home the claim that ancient Masonry consisted only of the three basic degrees, it was essential that what Masons wore should reflect that fact. If, as we know there were, Masons who attended Craft lodges sporting aprons that bore the insignia not only of such degrees as Mark, Ark and Royal Arch, but even of Knight Templar, Red Cross and Rose Croix, then it was essential in the Grand Lodge's eyes to stop that as soon as possible. The only way to do so was to devise the right and only forms of dress allowable.

The second factor was that just because the United Grand Lodge was now having to manage units that had had allegiances to differing Grand bodies, it had to assert its new control in some way that was not only permanent but visible. To remove the right of individual Masons to decide what kind of aprons they could wear, if they were able to afford them, was both a noticeable declaration of superiority whilst also claiming to be in accord with the same Grand Lodge's principles. If it was on the one hand desiring to admit into its lodges free men of every kind without political, religious, social or racial distinction, then it made sense to ensure that its member should all have commonly acknowledged forms of dress. There was no place for a division based on the ability of members to have variegated ritual garments.

It is as we consider all these aspects of what might be called the 1813 'revolution' that we can truly say, "Was there ever such a Change?"

What is the Point of other than the Craft degrees?

As may be apparent to anyone who may have consulted my curriculum vitae, I have some justification for claiming to know something about the degrees practised 'beyond the Craft'. The manner in which I came to be associated with so many and at a fairly early age is a story in itself but one that I cannot tell here. Suffice it to say that without, at that point of my life, understanding the relationship of all the steps I was taking, there were those who were, unbeknown to me, guiding my steps and making sure that I took them in the right direction and in the right order. It is only in my latter years when the whole business of learning ritual, ruling Masonic units and undertaking leadership over several of them is done that I can sit back and try to answer the question which this paper poses. It is a question that was actually put to me some three years ago and then repeated during the time that I was preparing this lecture for delivery. It is thus the response to a real concern felt by some Masons.

As I reflect on the path that I have taken I can only say that at this point I have a sense of having made a long journey in which all the parts seem to fit. I feel this so confidently that I was about to respond to a request by some of my present colleagues in York to write them a paper in which I could explain how the different degrees and Orders fit together. It was then that the second query on this paper's topic came up and I hope that what I say here may meet both purposes. If it does not my York brethren will have to wait for something else.

What also spurred me on was an experience I had in visiting the Grand Scribe E of the Supreme Grand Charter of Scotland at the end of last year. We had been talking about the subsidiary degrees that now lie under the care and authority of that Grand

Chapter. He told me that one of the European Grand Lodges had now decided that it was time to prepare for the task of allowing their growing number of members to complete the experience that they had so far had in practising the Craft degrees, including of course the Installation of a reigning Master. What they needed was advice on the most satisfactory way of introducing the Holy Royal Arch. It is worth noting here that though this foreign Constitution is in full and happy relationship with the United Grand Lodge and Supreme Grand Chapter of England they went to Scotland for this purpose.

What I found to be of interest and of relevance to this paper is the fact that, faced with such an enquiry, the Supreme Grand Chapter of Scotland was not inclined to say: "Well, we suggest that you do it just as we do", but took a quite new line. They said: "If you are now ready to take this step into what is undoubtedly the ancient completion of the Craft steps then we want to suggest that you do what we would like to do if we were able, but are not, and that is to start afresh. We would adopt the following sequence: Mark: Super Excellent Master: Knight of the East: Royal Arch: Knight of the East and West: Grand High Priest or Installation degrees. That, we feel, would more correctly complete the Masonic story."

It is not fitting for me to comment here on what may or may not be the correctness of this suggestion. All that I can do is remark that in the mind of these senior Scottish Masons there was a place for the degrees **after** the Craft and the events, especially of the Master Mason's degree, required the best possible succession of other steps to bring it to a satisfactory conclusion.

That this is not just wilful irresponsibility on the part of the Scots is made abundantly clear by looking at the stance of the older Grand Lodges in regard to other than the normal three degrees. All of them, as we well know, accept that in a significant sense, a Master Mason is not really a completed Mason until he has been through the Chair of his lodge. Whether or not such a step is constitutionally regarded as a degree or not – though every Constitution requires an Installed Master to take an obligation, to receive secrets and to hear some kind of historical explanation of his new status – this is not in any way thought to be completely unnecessary. On the contrary, the brother who does **not** proceed to the Chair is usually the odd one out. This is not said in any sense of disparagement of such a decision, but the truth of Masonic history is that when a brother has been a Fellow (and was in earlier days called a Master) of the Craft then he was eligible for the Chair of a true Master Architect (hence the tools of the present 3°) and it was then the case that he could learn about the remaining 'Mason Word' that was the climax of all Freemasonry.

In England in the 18th century, and even in the Chapters reluctantly allowed by the Premier Grand Lodge, it was the rule that no-one could proceed beyond the Craft unless he had completed the step of occupying the Craft Lodge Chair. It was only after 1836 that the significant change was made which allowed 3° Masons to proceed to Exaltation in the Holy Royal Arch order. This was the natural and logical outcome of the agreement reached between the uniting Grand Lodges by the Act of Union in 1813 – Pure and Ancient Masonry consists only in the degrees of Craft Masonry together with the Holy Royal Arch. As far as England was officially concerned, a very effective compromise had been reached – the Craft's pre-eminence had been re-affirmed – which meant that the protagonists of the Premier Grand lodge were vindicated – whilst the place of the Royal Arch as a necessary adjunct to the Craft was recognised – which pleased the members of the Antients Grand Lodge. Now that the Royal Arch is administered as a separate entity in England, albeit by the same permanent officers, there has to be some recognition that whatever the 'technical or legal' connection with the Craft may be those who enter the 'supreme degree' of the Holy Royal Arch are stepping beyond the bounds known only by those who remain 3° or even just Installed Master Masons. Further, the Royal Arch Mason knows soon enough that he has taken a substantial step forward beyond the 3° and in any case has three more steps to take before he can encompass the whole of the new Order he has entered. Yet all this, states the Act of Union, is a necessary completion of the Craft. One of the answers to my first question has already been given. The Craft degrees in England are deemed incomplete without at least the exaltation into, and occupying the Chairs of, the Holy Royal Arch.

In Scotland, the situation is somewhat different. Following the pattern of the Premier Grand Lodge of England, the Scottish Grand Lodge was for long adamant that Ancient Free and Accepted Masonry consisted of three degrees and no more. They too recognised that the Mastership of a lodge had somehow to be included in that categorical statement but every effort was made to prevent the same thing happening in Scotland that had occurred South of the Border. There the activities of the Grand Lodge of the Antients meant that such degrees as Mark Man and Mark Master, Passing the Chair, Super-Excellent Master, Royal Arch and even Orders of Chivalry were all able to be practised on the authority of the Craft Lodge warrant. This, they vowed in Scotland, must not happen. Then the problem arose. Certain very long-standing lodges proved beyond any shadow of a doubt that they had the established custom of conferring some kind of Mark ceremony on those who were Fellow of the Craft Masons. It might be done in a Master Masons' lodge but it was an ancient rite for all those who had proved themselves to be true Fellows. What could the Grand Lodge of Scotland do? Their decision was made more difficult in that, to avoid the English compromise, there had already been established a Supreme Grand Chapter which had happily taken under its wing the Mark degree. Yet the Grand Lodge could not allow the Grand Chapter to interfere in the life of the Craft Lodges by ruling their Mark ceremonies nor would the old Lodges concerned stomach any such interference. The Grand Lodge of Scotland accepted that whatever they professed about the Craft degrees (and the Installation) they now had to countenance the practice of the Mark in some form **within and as part of** old Craft working. The restriction of the Installation of a Master of a Mark Lodge to the authority of the Supreme Grand Chapter was as far as compromise in that country went. Again, however, we see that anyone who asks what is the point of the other than Craft degrees has to begin to recognise that even the best intentions of clear-minded Grand Lodges cannot be maintained. There is some point and purpose in the practice of what does not come strictly within the current definition of 'the Craft Degrees'.

In Ireland it looks at first as if the ideal situation has been achieved, for the Grand Lodge in that land controls only the Craft degrees and the Installation of a Master. Yet the very reasons for the setting up of a Grand Chapter there was because Irish lodges in the 18th century practised a whole range of degrees under a Craft warrant rather like their cousins, the Antients in England. In order to organise the range of degrees and bring some greater uniformity into Irish Masonry, especially when there were also Encampments and their subsidiary degrees, the Grand Chapter was instituted but so close had the Craft and other degrees been for so long that it was fully acknowledged in Dublin that there could be no such declaration as had been made in England or Scotland. The Grand Lodge may rule over the Craft degrees but no-one pretends that that in any way defines the sole importance of that basic branch of Freemasonry. The so-called 'other degrees' are still acknowledged as being important.

We thus find ourselves constitutionally in a situation where no-one categorically excludes the non-Craft degrees though there are different views as to how they should be regarded. What remains for us to do in this presentation is to answer two questions:

1. What has been and should be the continuing core of Speculative Freemasonry?
2. How do the other than Craft degrees fit or not into that definition?

These are big questions and I can only attempt my own answer to them. It is quite likely that others will have their own views on them and I can only hope that if that is the case we can begin to develop a useful debate. Let us begin to tackle the first issue.

1. The Core of Speculative Freemasonry

In defining this matter, there are, I believe, six stages:

a. We begin by joining the team of Masons who are engaged on the building of the Temple as envisaged by King Solomon, with the assistance of Hiram, King of Tyre. The latter provides not only essential materials but also some labour and in particular a Master-Craftsman who is skilled in forging metal, but also in the planning, designing and overseeing of the whole work. It is into the team that he directs that any new Mason is traditionally recruited and it is to learn the skills that he will be able to wield, and the tools that will enable him to perform, that the new apprentice commits himself to obligation. He soon realises that he is very much part of a team and that he has obligations of care and co-operation towards the other members of his lodge, as well as to the universal society of which he has become a member. He is put on his honour to maintain the principles of which he will now

91

increasingly become aware. He in entrusted with his first 'secrets'.

b. After a suitable interval which represents his apprenticeship he is considered for fuller admission into the society of Fellows of the Craft. He has to prove himself competent in the work that has already been entrusted to him but he has also to show that he is not only a mere 'hand' but has a mind that can create. He has to prepare his own pieces of work for building into the Temple and at some point that work has to be seen and judged suitable for the sacred purposes for which it is destined – no less than the Temple sanctuary. He is told of how Hiram the Master Architect has divided up the work into different classes of workmen, each under their Overseers or Harodim. He is taught that because the Temple was to be constructed 'in silence on the site', so the work produced by him and others had to be marked in order that it could be laid in place without hesitation and also that good work could be rewarded. He is even told where to go to receive his wages and how to request them. He is again warned that any who misuse their privileges will be punished and, as in his previous obligation, that there are comparable penalties. He is even introduced to the various sciences that enable him to be a true Master of the Craft.

c. His progress in participating in the work at the Temple site is such that he is now ready to be considered for a post of management, first as one of the Harodim but thereafter, if judged fit, to be an Architect Master, able to draw designs, lay schemes and manage the government of the work. He is even able to be considered as a possible future Hiram, the widow's son, but in order to attain that high status, he has to have learnt the secrets of a Master Overseer and rules over those, who, like himself have regularly produced marked work according to the plans of the Grand Master of the work, and become aware of the great responsibility that that demands. He will realise what is still required to complete the Temple building and he will be aware not only of the danger of over-ambition revealed by some Overseers but the disastrous results when some of those Overseers overstep the mark. The very Grand Master who is to be their and his pattern is murdered and only properly entombed after being fortuitously discovered. The Grand Master Hiram Abi's removal from the scene means that a substitute has to be found in order that the Grand Secret within a completed Temple can be maintained.

d. The Mason is now so competent as a ruler that he is selected to be Hiram's replacement and becomes Adoniram. He helps to complete the Temple with its final Arch and Solomon can dedicate the edifice assisted by the Priests, like Jachin, and in the presence of many Princes and Rulers, such as his ancestor, Boaz, was and including the Queen of Sheba. Adoniram joins the Kings in maintaining the Mason's Word in a sacred chamber beneath the Temple and order is maintained amongst the workmen.

e. Following the death of Solomon the kingdom is once more divided and eventually falls to the attacks of the Babylonians. The Grand Secret or Mason's Word is similarly dissipated and lost. The nobility and rulers of Israel are taken into captivity and it is only when Persia conquers Babylon that the opportunity arrives for a return to rebuild Jerusalem and the Temple. Men such as Ezra and Nehemiah undertake the first task and at last a Prince, Zerubbabel, aided by prophets, like Haggai, and the priesthood, including Joshua Ben Jozedek, seek to undertake the rebuilding of the Temple. They are rebuffed by the local pagan rulers and only after Zerubbabel has appealed successfully to Cyrus can he come back and uncover the sacred chamber and the lost Mason's Word. All who assist the Sanhedrim in its task are made Princes and Rulers.

f. The ultimate discovery is that the Mason's Word has a threefold form. All those who are deemed worthy of knowing it as Rulers and Princes are made privy to it and not simply Kings and their intimates as previously. Knowing the Word is of course not enough. Those who know it are expected to exemplify their knowledge by the kind of lives they live in society generally. For their guidance and instruction biblical and historical figures are portrayed and imitation of their good deeds encouraged – just as was recommended when Hiram Abi first suffered. When the good Mason has lived respected and died regretted his whole life is complete.

2. How do the non craft degrees fit into that pattern?

Beginning of course with the recognition in the above survey that the Apprentice, Fellow Craft and present Master Mason degrees are already there, it can, I hope be seen how naturally, as in those old Scottish lodges, the Fellow of the Craft led to the Mark Man (receiving your mark) and the Mark Master (taught how to receive wages and present your masterpiece as a keystone), which latter skill meant that you were deemed fit to rule over a Fellow Crafts' lodge before you became an Excellent Mason as a ruler over a Master Masons' lodge. Having so proved your worth as a ruler, you can the better take part in the completion of the Temple, though the Most Excellent Master degree fully entitles you to use your keystone masterpiece as part of that final Arch-raising occasion and enables you to appreciate the Arch of the Rainbow which characterises the Royal Ark Mariner degree.

You are now about to be admitted to the secrets of the inner chamber of the Temple through the veils of the Super Excellent degree, but first the degree of Knight of the East prepares you for the return from the exile and the Royal Arch experience once you have reached Jerusalem. The Royal and Select Masters degrees tell of the trials experienced in seeking to restore the Temple and Jerusalem whilst some of the Allied degrees complete the story and also belong to the progress to the Arch chairs.

It is as one becomes a complete Ruler and Prince that the degrees of Rose Croix, Knight Templar, Red Cross of Constantine and Royal Order of Scotland have their own lessons to convey whilst the Knight Templar Priest and the Order of the Secret Monitor provide biblical patterns for our behaviour that we should be honoured to follow. The Operative degrees only serve to underline the story of what it is to be a Temple Mason who might eventually become a Grand Master Mason.

If that seems to be fitting the existing degrees to a contrived pattern then I have to say that that is how it may appear because of the form of Freemasonry that followed the early severance of the full Master's Part from the other sections of the original Craft ceremonies. When in 1813 in England, and shortly afterwards in Scotland and Ireland, Grand Lodges sought to limit their activities to what **they deemed** to be 'the Craft Degrees', then it was bound to look as if everything else was simply an addition and a doubtful addition at that. What I have been trying to say in this paper is that that is a faulty way of considering the question. To put it another way, in the so-called non-Craft degrees we have fuller parts of what was originally the 'whole Craft working'. If you do not participate in the non-Craft degrees then you are actually missing out on some of the original Freemasonry to which you are the rightful heir. That is their point and that is why I for one am so grateful that I was introduced to them. I am, I would claim, a truly instructed and fully fledged Craft Mason. I know where I came from and I know where I have arrived – at the Ne Plus Ultra of the ancient Craft.

Adventures of a Masonic Author

The title of this talk may have given some of you pause for thought. How is it possible for there to be any adventures for a Masonic author? Hasn't all the ground been covered that could possibly have been a subject for discovery, so what is there to have any adventures about? In any case, what kind of adventures can there possibly be in our field of study? One could understand the author of fiction or travel books, of biography or of some fresh scientific investigation having an adventure or two in the course of their researches. Indeed, as an author in at least two of these fields as well I can certainly testify to the truth of that understanding. But Masonic material? How can that be? Well, I hope that what I am able to share with you this evening may help alter any such doubts that some of you may have and indeed encourage another amongst you to enter into the delights of adventure that I have already experienced.

Let me begin in a place of which I am an enthusiastic devotee. I refer to Corfu. For years I used to hear about this island at the Southern end of the Adriatic without ever imagining that one day I would know it well. Yet in the last 25 years I have visited it often, whether as a clergyman, being the English Chaplain in Corfu Town, or else just going to stay with friends there as a tourist. On my third visit, I became aware of the local Freemasons and was able to win the trust and confidence of the Greek brethren who meet in the capital. I would attend their meetings, where incidentally, all the ceremonies are conducted in their own language and I began to appreciate their different way of doing things. I learnt about their island history, which is a long and varied one, but even more about their Masonic history, which was largely unknown and wholly unwritten. I began to hear about certain figures and traditions and to wonder where all the evidence for this might be found.

As an author and Masonic student I began to make enquiries about their past, especially in the British period of rule there (1815-1856). I looked at material in the Grand Lodge library in London as I then lived there and on a visit in 1982 I daringly asked the Corfiot Masons if there was possibly somewhere in their premises where old documents might have been kept. "Nai", (Yes), I was told, "we do have two rooms up the old staircase but what is in them we have no idea. You are quite free to look at them if you wish and perhaps you will tell us if you find anything interesting."

There followed a week of pure adventure – back into an hitherto untouched past. Here were the minute books, certificates, warrants, bye-laws, lists of members (with their occupation), medals, dispensations and other records of Greek lodges that had been held here. Yet that was not all. Here too were the records of the previous British and even earlier French lodges that had first established Masonry in this ancient place. It was pure treasure trove – and clearly it was high time for it to be found and retrieved. Some of the documents were beginning to show the effects of damp, many of them were lumped together in disordered piles and several of the manuscripts had handwriting that was beginning to fade. I had the excitement and privilege of beginning to recover some 150 years of unknown past history. Not inappropriately, the name of the last British lodge that met here was called Phoenix. For this is an adventure that has not yet finished. Through the efforts of a native Greek Freemason who travels regularly to our Q.C. Lodge in London, Andreas Rizopoulos, I have been able to add another chapter to the chequered history of the Craft in Greece. A recent edition of our Q.C. Transactions shows what has already begun to emerge.

My own historical studies on Corfu (about which, incidentally I am trying to write an historical novel) had centred on its most well-known but also infamous governor, Sir Thomas Maitland, known locally as 'King Tom', and these studies led me to the other island that he also found time to govern simultaneously . . . The Mediterranean island of Malta. On my first visit there I just had to visit the old lodge room and library in Valetta and thus to see where Freemasonry had been practised in that no less ancient port. I was received with much fraternal warmth amongst the English-speaking brethren. On my revealing an interest in the many unusual items that were strewn around the cases in the lodge library, I was asked if I would consider arranging and cataloguing them afresh so that, in future, the lodge members and any visitors would better appreciate the treasures that this lodge held.

The job took me three days and then, as a reward, I was allowed to see the main content of their safe – the first minute book of the Lodge of St. John and St. Paul, dated 1805. I was again looking at material that had rarely been studied before and the thrill of seeing renowned English Freemasons – the Earl of Moira and Waller Rodwell Wright to mention but two – working here in this outpost of a growing Empire was reward indeed. The lasting result of that visit was a lecture that I still sometimes give called "The First Freemasons of Malta" – and I am not talking about the Knights of St John. To discover the differences and the peculiarities of those early 19th century lodge days was another adventure in itself.

Of course, being recognised as a Masonic author does not always make for a quiet life. I sat one afternoon in what was then my London office, discharging my daily avocation, when the Grand Secretary of England, then fairly new, rang me up. "Please help me", was the cry. "There is a Lodge Centenary meeting at 5pm today and the Assistant Grand Chaplain who should have given the Oration at this Jewish Lodge has just let us know that he cannot get there. Can you take his place?" "Well," I replied, "I would be willing to but I have no regalia with me in

Town, I am at present sitting here in a very light grey suit a blue shirt and brown shoes and I have no idea which lodge it is nor do I carry round a readymade address." That was enough for another adventure to begin.

In no time at all I was assured that regalia fitting my station would be awaiting me in the lodge ante-room, money was available for me to buy a white shirt and black tie, and even black shoes if I desired, and I need not attend until 5.30pm (after the lodge had opened and the minutes had been read) so I had a **little more time** to compose the necessary Oration and he told me in his usual crisp naval manner something about the Lodge that I was to attend. The time was 3.00pm.

By 5.30pm, I was entering the lodge room preceded by an Assistant Grand Director of Ceremonies. I was still in a light grey suit and with brown shoes. I had purchased a white shirt and black tie and an address was in my hand. I felt odd, but the Lodge had been alerted to the situation and their welcome and appreciation were of the warmest. All seemed to go off satisfactorily, and in my home today there is a cut glass goblet which still reminds me of the event. It may be a joy to compose but that is one adventure I have no early desire to repeat. On the other hand it was touching, just a fortnight ago, to meet a Brother in Surrey who told me that he had been in that very audience and that he will never forget what I said and the effect that my "adventure" had on the Masons wanting to commemorate their Lodge achievement.

By the same token I was able, just a little time ago, to enjoy another adventure. I was, 25 years ago, invited as Assistant Grand Chaplain and Past Provincial Grand Chaplain of Sussex, to assist at the Consecration of the Hoove Lodge in Brighton. I was expected of course to give the Oration. I did so and, as my custom has always been, I gave the text of the Oration to the Lodge because I never use any such material twice. It was and is to be theirs alone.

Happily they kept it in their records and when they were planning what to do for their commemoration of the first 25 years of the Lodge's life they asked me if I would come to Brighton and deliver that same Oration to the present members of Hoove Lodge. That was what I did. To share with a whole new generation of Masons something that only their Founders had actually heard was a real adventure. I am grateful that health and strength have enabled me to do what many might never have had the opportunity to fulfil. To repeat the actual event of a quarter of a century ago was adventure indeed.

Another adventure was the visit I paid in 1988 to the Masonic Hall at Old Elvet in Durham. I was in the midst of researching material for the series of books I have now had published on the Masonic Halls of England, including the North. I had been assured that I could visit the Hall that night and see, as well as photograph, its treasures. These include the outsize, specially designed, Master's chair of the actor, William Kemble, who was over 18 stone and big with it, and a pair of Masonic 'baptismal' aprons which are in a surprisingly good condition after 200 years. To my dismay I found that a meeting of the august University Lodge, the only lodge in that building to wear evening dress, was taking place and my projected tour of the building was therefore limited.

Having come a long way with my camera to see this old Hall I was very reluctant to depart empty handed but as I mounted the fine Grand Staircase, dressed in a sandy T-shirt, light blue trousers and sandals, I was rightly challenged by the Lodge Tyler as to who I was. I told him I was the Grand Chaplain of England but was researching for a book on Masonic Halls. I said I would just photograph a few items and then wait for the Lodge to go to refreshment so that I could see the great oak-timbered Temple. The Tyler reported to the Lodge and an order came out that I should do them the honour of joining them. The Tyler was to lend me his Past Master's regalia and gloves and then to announce me. I was duly admitted, with T-shirt and all, and made surprisingly welcome. I shall be speaking to the Installed Masters of Durham soon and I am sure that there will still be someone who will rib me about a very bizarre 'adventure' indeed. I must hasten to add that they even invited me to dinner as well.

I can never forget the adventure of first visiting Tapton Masonic Hall, Sheffield, and starting what has ever since been an admiring appreciation of its treasures. The portraits on the Landing upstairs are one of the best examples of the development of the Collarette and Collar to be found anywhere in the Craft. Yet some halls do not preserve and honour their treasures as they do. The adventure of discovering what is hidden can sometimes be very exciting indeed.

I recall a trip to North Wales for the material needed for yet another book on Masonic Halls there in that Principality. I reached Denbigh, the birthplace of General Gordon, and searched for the Masonic Temple. It is tucked away near the upper gate of the walls that still surround this ancient town and is in a converted Chapel. Generally it is well maintained, but after I had looked at the main rooms I asked what was in the little room off the landing. "Just junk", I was told, and that, they thought, was that. That is a phrase that I have heard so often that it simply invited more investigation on my part. I asked them to let me see. There was indeed a large wooden box. We lifted the lid and there was 'junk' – or was it? We pulled the things out and immediately there appeared a sort of grey canvas suit with pyjama-type trousers and a top with a flap over the left breast area. 'Whatever is this?', I was asked, and **I was** the visitor. I explained, for I had read the lodge history before arriving. "Do you recall that in about 1830 there was the record of having bought a new suit for the initiate?" "Yes", was the reply, "and we often thought that was unusual to buy a suit for the candidate". "Well, this is it, I told them". "The suit was not for wearing *outside* but for use in the ceremonies. This is what your predecessors wore in the 19th century for admission to the degrees. I suggest you get it cleaned and displayed for present and future members to see and learn from." They were impressed and so we rummaged further.

There was a roll at the bottom of the box. We got it out and unrolled it on the landing. It was the first banner of the Lodge dating from about 1795. 'We wondered where this had got to', was their cry. I urged them to write to the Grand Librarian in London so as to discover how to preserve this symbol of their origins, and to frame it for posterity. They were delighted and realised why I was so insistent on opening storeroom doors and the lids of boxes.

The same was true in Scotland. I was in the Kingdom of Fife at the Masonic Hall of Newburgh. My object in visiting here was mainly to examine a huge mural that covers the East wall of the Temple behind the Master's throne. Discovering that and a similar mural in a Dundee Lodge room was adventure enough but here in Newburgh there was more. I dragged myself away from the stunning array of figures on the wall and looked at other items. By now they knew me and as I gazed at a picture of the old-time Tyler of this lodge, dressed in tricorn hat, light blue jacket, yellow waistcoat and blue and yellow striped stockings, they remarked, "We thought you would like that. It's as good as the one at Perth." "Yes," I replied, "but the people in Perth still have the original clothing." (They have put it on a tailor's dummy and set it by the lodge doorway.) "Well, sadly, we don't have ours anymore but at least we know what he looked like."

A few minutes later, I asked them what was in the glass case that was attached to the wall above where the Secretary sat. You can guess what they said. Yes: "Junk, only junk, and we haven't looked in it for years." I got them to open it, to remove the old summonses, the odd jewels, the Charity Association reports, even a few old Year Books of the Grand Lodge of Scotland, and then . . . a light blue jacket, a yellow waistcoat and even a pair of blue and yellow striped stockings. "Ah, noo", they exclaimed, "Just fancy that. We **have** the Tyler's outfit after all." Well, they don't just have the hat, but when I next take my wife to Scotland, I want her to see the mural and I am hoping to see the suit on another dummy at Newburgh. Then my adventure will have been really worthwhile.

Just one more story before I close. This time, we go 'down under' to Adelaide in South Australia. I was on my first lecture tour there four years ago when the Grand Secretary of the State Grand Lodge took me on a visit to the Grand Temple and its many rooms. What struck me at once was that so many things seemed the wrong way round. The candlesticks were on the left of the pedestals and the pillars on the right. The ashlars were at the North- and South-West corners of the carpet and the winch was at the foot of the Master's pedestal. Even the banner was behind the Senior Warden's chair whilst the D.C. sat where you would expect the S.D. to be and the Deacons were on the left of the W.M. and the S.W. It was most odd and I dared to query it all with the Grand Secretary. "How strange of you to remark", he answered, "for surely this arrangement was brought here by one of our founding English Masons. What can be wrong with it?" What is certain is that because the Grand Lodge rooms are arranged like that, every other lodge room in the State has to be the same. There are no variations allowed.

It still puzzled me as I went to lecture in one of the rooms out of town. There I was shown into an ante-room with a rogues' gallery. You know, all the pictures of the Past Masters: in this case from about 1850 onwards. As I was examining the oldest ones, one of the local Masons caught my arm. "Do you notice," he said, "that the oldest pictures are back to front. Some of those pioneers didn't know how to develop their pictures right. That's why they look odd with their jewels on the opposite side to the usual." Surely, I then thought, that could be why the lodge rooms are arranged as they are. A pioneer brought a negative or a wrongly taken picture from Britain and that was used as the pattern. It might be wrong, but that is the way that South Australian Masons arrange their lodge rooms. Well, it was a nice theory, but it was wrong, and it took another adventure into our Masonic tradition for this author to find the right answer.

The answer has come by my now having begun to live in the Province of Yorkshire, North and East Riding. Some of the lodges that are in the North of that Province have, would you believe, all the features that are now in Adelaide expect for the positions of the Deacons. When I ask the brethren there why this was they could only give me the usual reply: it always has been so. What now does seem possible is that brethren from Teeside were amongst those first Masonic emigrants to South Australia and they set out their lodge room as they were accustomed to do. The Grand Secretary was absolutely right.

Worshipful Master, I have surely said enough to prove my point. In this part-time occupation of Masonic author there is adventure and discovery in abundance. What is so pleasing is that the travels and surprises still continue . . . and there is plenty for others to share in, if only they are so inclined.